# TO THE FRONT AND BACK

## FOUR AND A HALF YEARS IN THE LIFE

## OF AN INFANTRYMAN

PETER KENT

ISBN
0-9554891-0-5
978-0-9554891-0-5

First published in 2007 by Peter Kent, 124 Whalley Drive, Bletchley, Milton Keynes, Buckinghamshire. MK3 6HU.

Printed by Parchment Printers (Oxford) Limited, Crescent Road, Cowley, Oxford. OX4 2PB.

*For Mum and Dad*

*With Love*

# CONTENTS

# FOREWORD

There is no shortage of accounts of those men who fought in the First World War. Many of these are about the men who never came home and are all the more poignant because of this.

For many families, life before 1914 was not easy, but at least in many rural communities, there was a kind of social cohesion based around hearth and home. The seasons, through the church and festivals, were celebrated with enthusiasm and a real sense of pleasure. It is remarkable that so many men readily stepped into the unknown of military life when the call came. That they had the resilience and fortitude to see the war through is even more remarkable.

Private George Sidney Kent was one of these and, happily, returned to his hearth and home. Almost ninety years on, his son Peter has used both skill and imagination in recreating the story of his father's military life from a few brief diary jottings. It is a story worth reading not least because it represents the experience of so many men of that war. That it was a labour of love there is no doubt: the dedication "For Mum and Dad with love" says it all.

Dino Lemonofides

# INTRODUCTION

*** The soldier's own diary 1915**
*** Great War medals**
*** A collection of photographs**
*** Personal documents relevant to The Great War….**

These were the possessions of my late father that I am extremely privileged to own, and motivated me to research his active service. Although his diary was written with pencil and now faded, it has been possible to read all but a few words of his brief daily entries.

My father's life was tragically cut short just one month prior to my eleventh birthday; there was never the opportunity for my late brother and me to talk with him, or learn of his experiences during that era of his life. This family loss further prompted my thoughts and ultimately provided an important part of my family history research.

When commencing my research I had little information about The Great War, but it was not my intention to consider the strategies or technicalities of war. I simply wanted to follow my father's footsteps through the four and a half years of his service.

During a visit to the Regimental Museum in Oxford I met volunteer archivist Richard Jeffs who provided trench maps which were to prove invaluable, together with other extremely helpful information. I then obtained books relevant to my research.

Slowly a picture evolved of the horrors the men in the front line experienced; they seem unreal to us today. From water logged trenches where rats fed on corpses and the clothes of the living became infested with lice, my father and his comrades went *over the top* to face the unknown and possible death from a sniper's bullet. Visits made to the relevant theatres of war in Belgium, France and Italy were emotional, but assisted me to form a picture of those horrors encountered.

This book is intended to be my personal research into the war my father experienced.

## ACKNOWLEDGEMENTS

Special thanks are due to my wife Jean for her encouragement, help and patience whilst frequently rescuing me at the keyboard. I acknowledge the invaluable help received from the late Richard Jeffs, archivist at The Oxfordshire and Buckinghamshire L.I. Regimental Museum, for sharing his enthusiasm and supplying trench maps with relevant information to my research. More recently I have received continuing help and support from Dino Lemonofides, archivist at the Museum. I am extremely grateful to Dino for writing the foreword. Much of the research and information has been based on my father's diary 1915, The Battalion War Diaries and records at the Regimental Museum in Oxford, The Centre for Buckinghamshire Studies in Aylesbury, and various books. In particular I acknowledge Captain Wright's book documenting The First Bucks Battalion 1914-1919 from his personal memories during The Great War. This has been an important source of information. My thanks to Stefania Rigoni and Maria Vittoria Carli at The Tourist Information Offices, Asiago. I acknowledge with thanks my friend Pat Osborn for reading my typescript. And finally, my very special thanks to my father for the legacy he left that compelled my research and tell his story of the war he knew.

I further acknowledge copyright holders authorising reproduction of photographs and illustrations. The Imperial War Museum London, cover photograph reference Q70167, and the silhouette image heading each chapter; The Centre for Buckinghamshire Studies, photograph D 133/38, page 5; The Commonwealth War Graves Commission, aerial photograph Tyne Cot Cemetery between pages 84 & 85, and photograph of Boscon Cemetery page 89; Professor Richard Holmes, maps of The Somme Battlefield page 23, and The Ypres Salient page 40; The late Richard Jeffs, map of 48th Division trenches Asiago, between pages 50 & 51; The Oxford and Bucks Light Infantry Museum, photograph typical British Tommy page 24; Wilfred Halsey, photograph of "A" Company, First Bucks Battalion between pages 8 & 9; Ted Smith, personalised map of Ploegsteert Wood between pages 12 & 13; The Living Archives, quote from Hawtin Mundy's memoirs, page 17; Betty Turner, First Bucks Battalion Christmas menu 1917, page 48; Studio Grafico Renzo Matino, Schio, Italy, map page 46; Azienda di Promozione Turistica Altopiano di Asiago, Italy, map page 49.

Chapter One

# EARLY YEARS

My father was born on 3 January 1894, the eldest of three children born to Sidney George and Kate Kent. The family home was in Moat Lane Cottages, Aston Abbotts six miles north-east of Aylesbury in the county of Buckinghamshire. On 12 March 1894 he was christened George Sidney Kent.

In 1899 a sister Edith Mary was born followed by a brother Harry William in 1900. Sidney and Kate were members of the Primitive Methodist Chapel, and regularly attended services on Sundays. Their children were therefore brought up in a Christian home and attended Sunday school.

Regretfully I have little knowledge of my father's early years, but his formal education until the age of thirteen or fourteen was gained at the small Church of England School in Aston Abbotts. The work in his school drawing books during 1904-1906 indicates that he was a practical person who would possibly use those skills in future employment. However when leaving school he followed the family tradition and became an "ag. lab." (agricultural labourer). His early years were centred on family and village life. Like all young lads mischief would have been a part of that life, possibly resulting in some form of punishment.

My father possessed a fine bass voice, which was recognised in the Aston Abbotts area as he sang at Church and social concerts. I have memories of his voice whilst standing next to him in Chapel during Sunday evening services. I recall hearing, some time after his death that it would have been possible for him to follow a career as a singer. From browsing through early cricket scorebooks I am aware that he played cricket for Aston Abbotts; matches that were played against neighbouring villages on Saturday afternoons.

Following demobilisation in 1919 my father first resumed life as an agricultural labourer, but later followed a new career within the building industry until his untimely death in 1945.

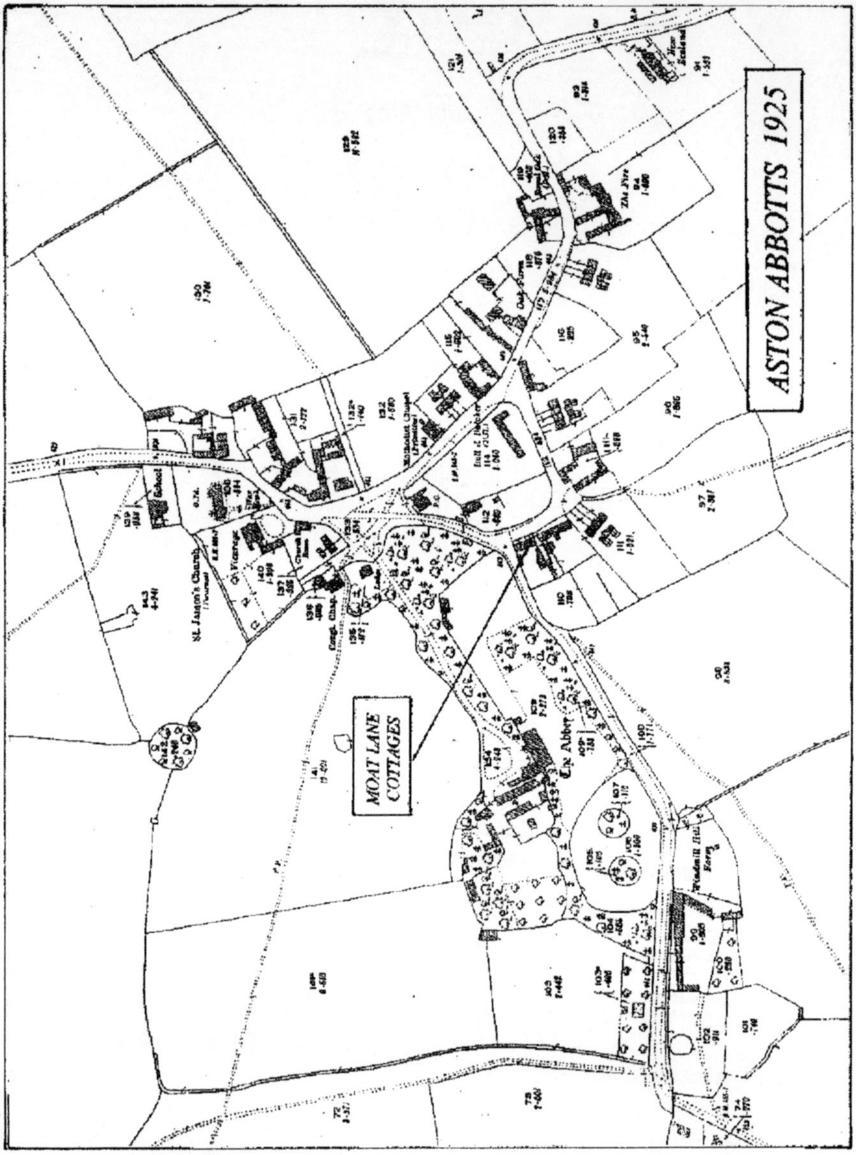
ASTON ABBOTTS 1925
MOAT LANE COTTAGES

My Father c 1910

## Chapter Two

# A NEW LIFE BEGINS

In 1914 unrest hung over Europe and war seemed inevitable as Germany invaded Belgium and Northern France. Britain issued an ultimatum to Germany threatening counter attack if they pursued these hostilities. The ultimatum expired at 11.00 p.m. on 4 August, but Germany remained silent. *WE WERE AT WAR.*

The regular army was mobilised and moved into France heading east to assist in the defence of Belgium and France. At that time no conscription existed in this country, but during late August the Minister for War, Lord Kitchener appealed for volunteers. Posters then appeared around the country and thousands of men volunteered; they become known as Kitchener's Army.

My father responded to Kitchener's appeal and wrote in the front of his diary

*Enlisted in first Bucks Terrys 4 Sept 1914*

Still only twenty years old he was the first man from his home village to volunteer for active service. That day he must have left home as normal, presumed to be going to work, but instead patriotism influenced him to go to Aylesbury and enlist. Several years after his death I recall hearing that when he returned home after enlisting and told his mother she boxed his ears. But, it had been his decision and after accepting the King's Shilling, there could be no going back.

My father's reference to the First Bucks Terrys confirms it being a Territorial Battalion. Enlisting very early ensured he would be amongst the first detachment from that Battalion to enter the war, and referred to as the 1/1st Bucks, forming part of the British Expeditionary Force (BEF).

The Bucks Battalion Headquarters in Aylesbury was taken over by the County Territorial Association in 1909 when relocating from their original site in Marlow. Origins of the Bucks Battalion date back to 1859 and the formation of the Bucks Volunteer Rifle Corps.

Further branches opened in Aylesbury, Slough (then in Buckinghamshire), High Wycombe and Eton College. In 1875 these branches merged to form the First Bucks Rifle Corps, and for part of their training they were attached to The Oxfordshire Light Infantry. A later proposal for Bucks to merge and become the 4th Battalion of the Oxfordshire Light Infantry was strongly rejected. Finally a compromise was reached leading to the formation of the Oxfordshire and Buckinghamshire Light Infantry.

Bucks Battalion H Q, Temple Square, Aylesbury. c 1914

My father's diary then records

*was billeted at Bell hotel Aylesbury (an undated entry)*

*left Aylesbury 8 September arrived at Chelmsford*

Just four days after enlisting my father with other volunteers moved to Chelmsford. At the time it was assumed by many that the war would be over by Christmas. However, the authorities did not mention to which Christmas they referred. Others predicted that it would be the war to end all wars, but sadly history later proved both these theories incorrect.

My father would have known several of the local young men volunteering at that time, such as Frank Halsey and Albert Ellis both from Aston Abbotts who served with the 1/1st Bucks. Other local men included Fredrick Coleman from the neighbouring village of Wingrave, and Albert Reynolds from Rowsham. Towards the back of his diary he recorded two names and addresses, presumably other young men with whom he formed early friendships. These prompt the questions; *Did they intend to meet up after the war?* And of course, *Did those two other young men survive the atrocities they were to experience?*

Chapter Three

## TRAINING AT CHELMSFORD

Thousands of Territorial Infantry volunteers were based in Chelmsford at that time, it was therefore necessary for many to be billeted in private houses.

My father's diary undated entries state

*was billeted with Mrs Binns 8 Grove Road*

*Second billet with Mrs Groves 11 Springfield Road*

*Third billet with Mrs Harvey 8 Springfield Road*

Life in and around Chelmsford would have been vastly different from what my father had known in his home village. Training and discipline would now mould him and other young men for the eventual horrors they would face in the front line and trenches. He could not have realised then what lay ahead, but he had volunteered to serve King and Country. Undoubtedly further friendships would have been formed whilst in training and later, but sadly many would be severed as the war progressed.

The firing range, bayonet practice, skirmishing, trenching, route marches, guard duties, fatigues, inspections all became part of the daily routine, together with weekly Church parades.

Possibly the highlight for the soldiers during their time in Chelmsford would have been the visit by King George V on 14 October 1914. A Guard of Honour was formed as the King arrived in the town before he was driven to Highlands Park. Although only receiving twenty-four hours notice of the King's visit, approximately fifteen thousand soldiers assembled in Highlands Park where His Majesty spent two hours mingling and talking with the men.

A cause for resentment among those Territorials was the cancellation of their Christmas leave due to an invasion scare. Christmas lunch was provided in Chelmsford and believed to have been in the Corn Exchange.

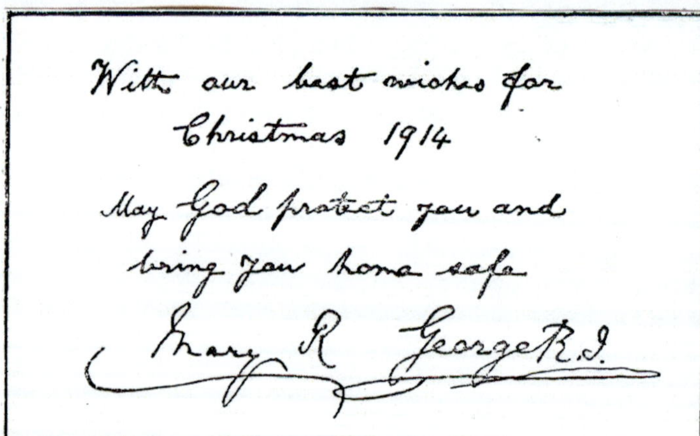


From my father's memorabilia

A personal card and message to all serving soldiers
from H M King George V and Queen Mary
Christmas 1914

From my father's memorabilia

Princess Mary's gift to all serving soldiers Christmas 1914
The brass tin contained a Christmas card, her personal photo and a selection from cigarettes, tobacco, small clay pipe and sweets

Doubtless my father would have preferred Christmas lunch at home with his family, but he would not have realised then that his next Christmas at home with them would be several years later.

Moving on to 1915 training continued but impatience crept in to the men's thoughts, now clearly focused on the front line. The war they thought could not be won without the First Bucks Battalion; doubtless this was the attitude of all Battalions in training at that time.

Early 1915 diary entries state

Tuesday 12 January, *Went home on leave*

Sunday 17 January, *Came back from leave*

Training continued through January, February and March.

Chapter Four

# PLOEGSTEERT WOOD, BELGIUM

During late March the news that had been awaited finally reached my father and his fellow soldiers. At 3.00 p.m on Tuesday 30 March 1915 the men paraded for the last time on the square, and marching to the railway station they entrained for Folkestone. From there they embarked on the Steam Ship *INVICTA* arriving in Boulogne at 11.00 p.m. A two-hour route march south brought them to Ostrehove camp where they spent what remained of the night. The strength of the Battalion at that time was 28 Officers and 916 other ranks including a Roman Catholic Chaplain.

At 3.00 p.m. next day they formed up and marched to Pont de Briques and their first experience of travelling on a French troop train, consisting of twenty cattle trucks. These trucks utilised for transporting the troops were normally identified to carry 40-50 Hommes or 8 Chevaux. The train hauled by a steam engine was quickly named "Puffing Billie". At Pont de Briques a machine gun section, batman and interpreter joined the Battalion, increasing their strength to 31 Officers and 1002 other ranks. Heading east an uncomfortable five hour journey terminated in Cassell at 11.00 p.m. followed by a three hour march to Terdeghem.

There they were billeted on farms, and although there was a supply of straw for *comfort* many chose to sleep outside. During that night the wind changed direction and in the morning the distant guns could be heard. My father and his mates realised they had arrived in the neighbourhood of war. Two further nights were spent at Terdeghem before the men marched on to billets along the Oultersteene-Bailleul Road (south-east of Méteren) where they spent two further nights. On 7 April the men marched through Bailleul and Armentières, then north into Belgium to Le Bizet for trench attachment with the 4th Division.

Next day each Company was attached to units within the 4th Division and instructed in the methods for holding trenches. During the hours of darkness guides accompanied their march forward to the trenches, where they spent two days in the front line and two days in support.

That would have been an unforgettable experience for my father and his mates, and often referred to as their *gunfire baptism.*

Entry in my father's diary Friday 9 April

*Went in the firing line*

It is impossible for us to fully appreciate what that experience was like. How could we? I have often wondered what my father would have told my brother and me.

On 17 April the Battalion arrived at Ploegsteert Wood and relieved the 1st Battalion Somerset Light Infantry in the support trench. The wood of about one square mile is located just north of Ploegsteert Village at the most southerly edge of the Ypres Salient and criss-crossed by paths and tracks. Many of the paths were given names making the soldiers feel *at home*; names included The Strand, Charing Cross, Fleet Street, Regent Street, Oxford Circus and Hyde Park Corner.

Hyde Park Corner c 1915

Houses behind the line near to St Yves were also given appropriate names; these included Hull's Burnt Farm, St Yves Post Office and Three Huns. The trenches most frequented by the Battalion were to the north-east of the wood and close to the small village of St.Yves, a section they alternated with the 1/5th Gloucesters, and consisting of sandbagged walls and duck-board bottoms. One lasting memory of their first experience in the trenches would undoubtedly have been the enormous amount of flies and the unforgettable smell. Moving between the wood and trenches could only be undertaken during hours of darkness.

However there existed in the Ploegsteert area a certain amount of fraternisation between the British and Germans, They referred to each other as Fritz and Tommy as they conversed across No Man's Land, a distance varying between one hundred and two hundred yards.

It was mainly along this area of the Western Front that the unauthorised Christmas truce of 1914 had taken place, although it was unacknowledged by the hierarchy of the British army. During Christmas morning the Germans began singing *Stille Nacht Heillig Nacht,* (Silent Night Holy Night) and the British joined in. The Germans responded, *We not shoot, you not shoot.* One German soldier sang Annie Laurie. Amazingly both armies left their trenches, laid down their guns and met in the centre of No Man's Land, where they exchanged presents including cigars, bully beef and even battledress buttons. An impromptu game of football was played, suggesting that neither army was there by choice. The men returned to their respective trenches and the war continued.

Diary entry Saturday 24 April 1915

*Went to Armentières for bath and change of underclothes*

It appears possible there was a brewery in Armentières as often they were utilised during the nights as communal baths. The huge vats no longer used for brewing provided *ideal bathing facilities* for the army. Water was not changed frequently and therefore it is not difficult to appreciate the importance of trying to be among the first to bath. It was not unusual following their bath that the men would be hosed down, presumably to cleanse their bodies of the stale bath water.

When not in the line my father would be in the wood or at Romarin about three miles to the west. Entries in his diary regularly refer to being in the trenches, on guard duties, fatigues, being on Church parade, and having inspections, including rifle, bayonet, own rations, and feet. He made occasional references to *rest*.

During the early hours of 1 May 1915 Private Albert Reynolds from Rowsham, less than two miles from my father's home was tragically killed in action. He was 19 years old, and been in the front line for just three weeks. Albert was one of thousands of young men who volunteered and served in "C" Company, 1/1st Bucks Battalion. He was laid to rest in Ploegsteert Wood Cemetery located in the centre of the wood. Two of his brothers also served during The Great War. It is conceivable that Albert's untimely death was the first of my father's mates to be killed in action.

Ploegsteert Wood Cemetery c 1915, 1/1st Bucks burials

265662 Pte. G.S. Kent

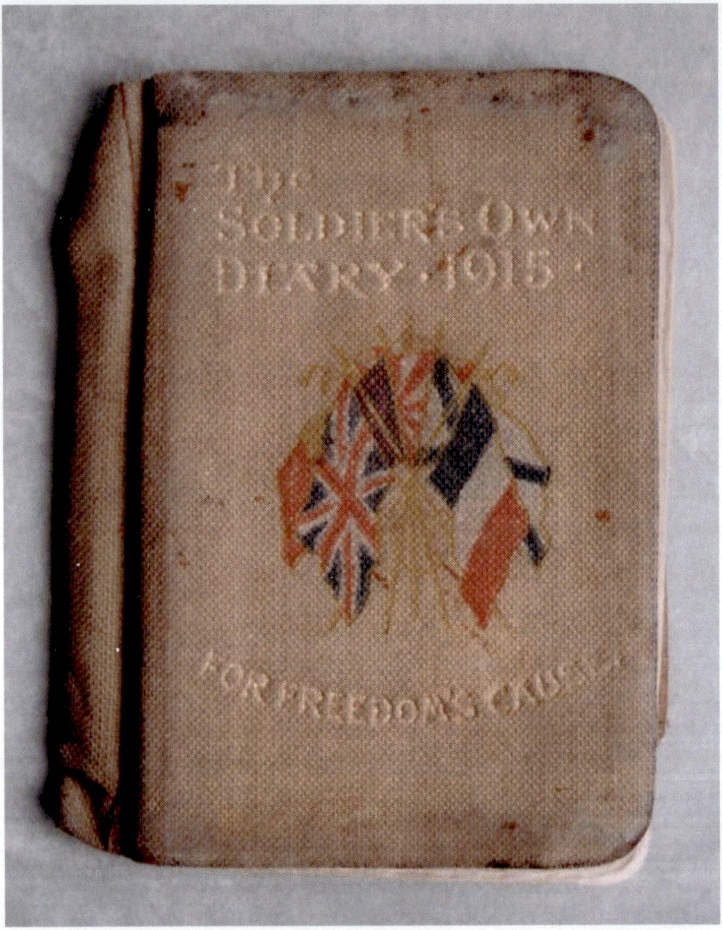


My Father's Diary

One fellow soldier from New Bradwell in Buckinghamshire, Hawtin Munday served in the 1/1st Bucks Battalion and made reference in his memoirs to sleeping during cold nights in Ploegsteert Wood.

*When you got there then you settled down and you had your groundsheet which you laid down. In my case I always used to do the same, because if your feet was warm you was warm all over. I always used to take me tunic off, put me feet in the sleeves, wrap the tunic round me legs and I used to put me boots at the top with me hat on me boots for me pillow and wrap a blanket round me and me greatcoat over the top and you could sleep as sound as a bell.*

Undoubtedly this would have been an experience shared by my father.

My father's diary entry for Sunday 30 May

*Anniversary, rest, trenches at night*

For some time I pondered over that reference to *Anniversary* and concluded he was referring to the Methodist Chapel Sunday School Anniversary at home. By tradition that special day was always held on the last Sunday during May. If he had not been in Ploegsteert Wood on 30 May he would certainly have been singing in the choir. From the trenches he possibly allowed his thoughts to wander and think of home.

His diary continues referring to his time in the trenches until 2 June then briefly states,

*Had the measles*

Diary entry Thursday 3 June

*Left for Romarin at night*

Three days were spent at Romarin but my father returned to Ploegsteert Wood on Monday 7 June and his diary entry reads,

*Went in the trenches at night*

The 1/1st Bucks, 1/4th Oxfords, 1/5th Gloucesters and 1/4th Royal Berks formed the 145th Brigade. The 143rd and 144th Brigades (each with four Battalions) completed the 48th South Midland Infantry Division, which until mid June was commanded by Major-General Heath, C.B. Illness then necessitated him handing over command of the Division to Major-General Sir Robert Fanshawe, C.B., D.S.O.

The Battalion's final short period in that area was spent in the Douve trenches facing Messines. During their first two and a half months in the front line the Battalion casualties were nine killed and sixty two wounded.

On 24 June the Division left the Ploegsteert area and moved south; then following a series of marches mainly during the night into Northern France. The route took them via Vieux-Berquin, Merville, and Busnettes to Allouagne just to the west of Béthune. A further move on 12 July led to bivouacs close to Nœux-les-Mines where the next two days were spent digging a new rear line.

Sudden orders were received on 16 July of another move. The Battalion marched through the night in a deluge of rain, to billets in Lières. It was customary for night marches to be carried out in silence. After about twenty minutes that night every man was thoroughly soaked, then word was passed down the line that the men were to be allowed to sing. I am certain my father would have welcomed that decision as he and his comrades sang lustily for the rest of the night. It is difficult to imagine the scene of a thousand men whilst marching with full pack, but seeing only the humour of the situation singing in torrential rain. Where next? they must have thought as rumours suggested The Dardenelles, Dunkirk, Ypres or Arras? On 19 July my father and his mates entrained at Berguette and leaving at 6.50 p.m. headed south to Doullens, and The Somme.

Diary entry Monday 19 July

*Arrived at 5 a.m. in wood had rifle bayonet and foot inspection*

Diary entry Tuesday 20 July

*Rest in wood at Sarton left at night*

Chapter Five

# THE SOMME

Marching on through Marieux, Coigneux and Sailly-au-Bois the men headed east to Hébuterne where the Division took over a section of the trenches from the French Army.

Diary entry Friday 23 July.

*Rifle inspection Rations scarce short of* ? (Entry unclear)

Diary entry Saturday 24 July

*Arrived at Hébuterne bath and left for Sailly-au-Bois to go in the trenches*

For several months now my father was in this area. His diary entries refer to duty in the trenches, fatigues, guard duty, inspections, route marches and listening post at night with an occasional reference to Church parades.

The 48th Division was amongst the first of the Divisions to arrive on the Somme in July 1915, and units from that Division started the Military Cemetery in Hébuterne. The inscription on the headstone of Lt. P D Doyne 1/4th Oxfords, k.i.a. 28 December 1915 proudly claims, *We are able.*

A sense of humour prevailed and became an important aspect of life for the British Tommy, and was evident during those early days on The Somme. When the Fifth Gloucesters took over the front line from the French they inherited a fine milking cow providing a daily supply of fresh milk.

Hébuterne Cemetery c1915

What luxury! The First Bucks relieved the Fifth Gloucesters in that section of the front line and were fortunate to be left with responsibility for the welfare of that regular supply of fresh milk.

That periodic change of ownership continued for several weeks and the cow was spared the frequent march back and forth between rest billets at Sailly and Hébuterne. However, after a while the First Bucks when vacating the front line only withdrew to the outskirts of Hébuterne, which then left the cow midway between the Fifth Gloucesters and themselves.

The irresistible temptation was for the First Bucks to obtain their supply of milk very early, leaving the cow dry for the Fifth Gloucesters at the normal milking time. Accusations then poured forth and the cow was never left again for the First Bucks. It was noted the continual marching back and forth proved too much for the cow who shortly afterwards was never seen again, she was presumed to have died from exhaustion.

The Battalion remained in the area around Hébuterne and towards the end of 1915 they alternated a section of the line with the 6th.Battalion, Gloucester Regiment. Each tour of duty was of eight days with rest billets in Couin about four miles west of Hébuterne.

Diary entry Thursday 30 September

*Rifle bayonet own rations inspection*

My father's entry here follows four days in the trenches, and his reference to the ration inspection was a frequent part of life in the front line. As well as his rifle, bayonet, ammunition, entrenching tool, greatcoat, groundsheet and first aid dressings he would have carried emergency rations. The latter would include a tin of Bully Beef, or Maconochie (a fat meat and vegetable stew) hard-tack biscuits and a flask of water. It was considered sufficient food was available to them whilst in the trenches, and therefore these rations were for emergency use only. No midnight feasts!

At times when fortunate to have a few surplus hard-tack biscuits a favourite recipe was trench pudding. The biscuits were pulverised into a cloth, then mixed with water and allowed to thoroughly soak. Ticklers jam was added, (they had a choice, either plum and apple or apple and plum). It was then cooked in their mess tins, and declared a tasty treat.

Heavy rains throughout November and continuing through December caused the trench walls to fall in, requiring continuous work in mud to keep

them clear. During the latter part of 1915 the entries in my father's diary became less frequent.
His last entry on Saturday 1 January 1916 briefly states

*Went in at night*

He must have referred to going in the trenches on New Years Day.

The Battalion War Diaries confirm they remained in the trenches until 3 January (my father's 22nd birthday) but they were reasonably quiet days. The Battalion moved back to Couin until 20 January, and then returned to Hébuterne relieving the 1/7th Worcesters in a different section of trenches during the following day.

From 1916 I have made reference to relevant entries from the Battalion War Diaries and other available records

*13.2.16 Granted 8 days leave to England from 31.1.16 to 7.2.16*

Although he had been just ten months on the Western Front it must have been paradise for my father to spend a few days at home with his family and friends. What picture would he have conveyed to them of his new life and experiences? He would have enjoyed real home cooking again and doubtless when leaving he would have returned to the front with a food parcel. Some soldiers received regular parcels from home and a marvellous camaraderie existed among them, as their food and cigarettes were frequently shared with their mates.

*12.2.16 Def. Vision, Adm.1/2 nd. 8th. Mid. F. Amb.*

*14.2.16 Ophthalmic, Adm.8th Mid.Cas. Cl. Stn.*

*16.2.16 Rejoined Battalion for duty*

These references to defective vision, ophthalmic, and admissions to the Midland Field Ambulance and Casualty Clearing Station suggest the cause may have been exposure to one of the many forms of gas used on the battlefields.

The Germans first used gas as a weapon in April 1915 and by the allies in September of the same year. Until the issue of gas helmets and gas masks during spring 1916 improvisation was made against the effects of a gas attack. A piece of cloth or an old sock would be soaked in urine; this was then secured around the face to provide a mask covering the nose and mouth. It was a crude deterrent with limited success, but what was the alternative?

During late February heavy snow fell and continued for several days. When possible some relaxation and active sport was encouraged, and during late March all companies were resting in Sailly-au-Bois. Football was a favourite amongst the sports available. On 23 March the finalists of The Fanshawe Cup were the 1/7 th Worcesters and 1/1 st Bucks. The result would have been a disappointment to my father as they were beaten by Two goals to Nil, but it had provided a welcome interlude from the trenches.

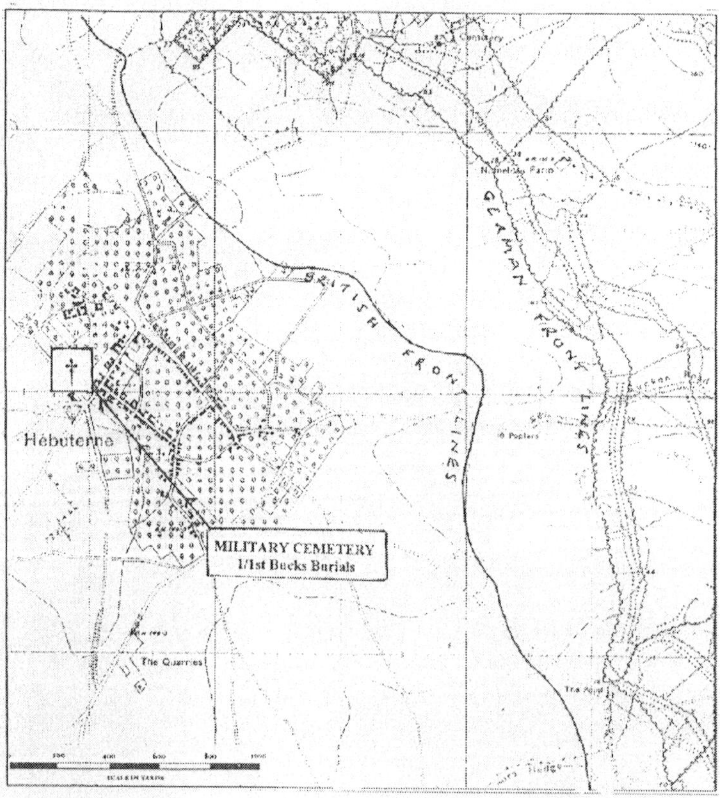

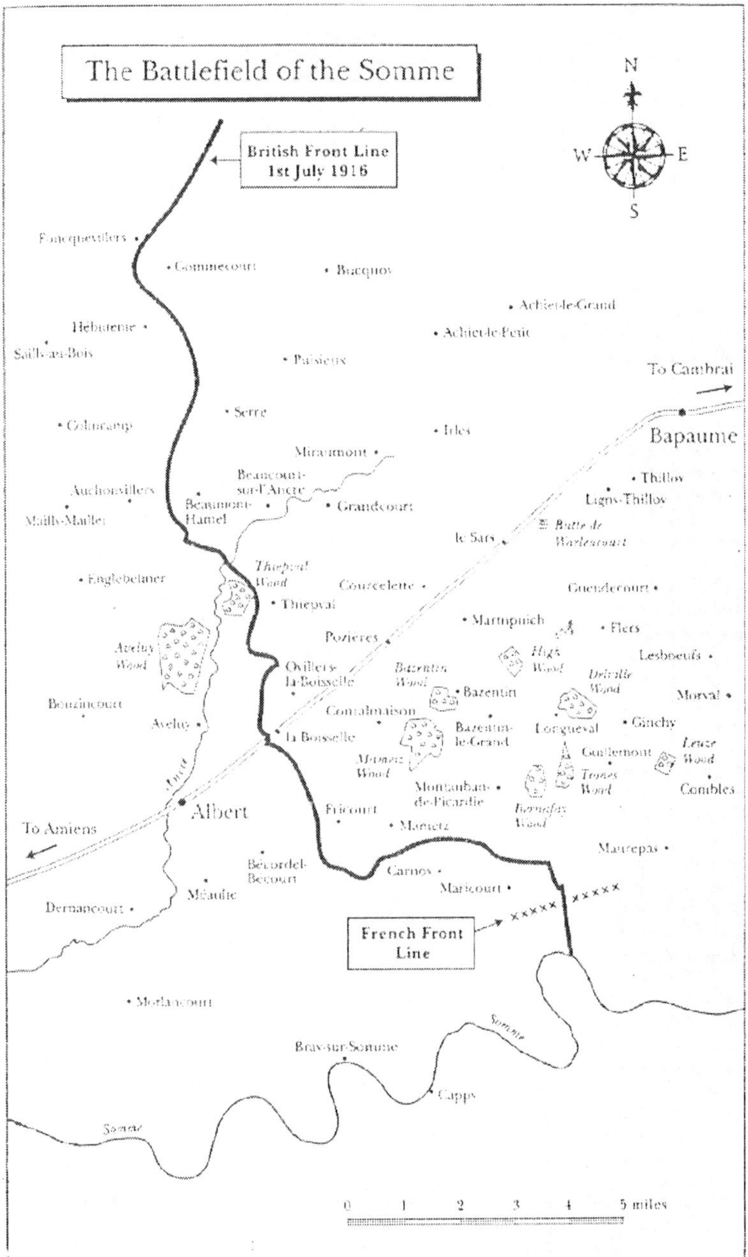
The Battlefield of the Somme
N
W
E
S
British Front Line
1st July 1916
Bucquoy
Achiet-le-Grand
Achiet-le-Petit
Hébuterne
Puisieux
To Cambrai
Serre
Bapaume
Miraumont
Thilloy
Ligny-Thilloy
Grandcourt
Beaumont-Hamel
Beaucourt-sur-l'Ancre
le Sars
Butte de Warlencourt
Thiepval Wood
Thiepval
Courcelette
Gueudecourt
Martinpuich
Flers
Pozieres
High Wood
Lesboeufs
Aveluy Wood
Ovillers-la-Boisselle
Bazentin Wood
Delville Wood
Bazentin
Morval
Contalmaison
Bazentin-le-Grand
Longueval
Ginchy
Aveluy
La Boisselle
Guillemont
Leuze Wood
Mametz Wood
Trones Wood
Montauban-de-Picardie
Combles
Albert
Fricourt
Mametz
Bernafay Wood
To Amiens
Maurepas
Carnoy
Maricourt
Méaulte
Dernancourt
French Front Line
Morlancourt
Somme
Bray-sur-Somme
Cappy
Somme
0 1 2 3 4 5 miles

During spring 1916 steel helmets were issued for the first time. It is difficult to appreciate that until then the men went *over the top* with no more to protect their heads than cloth caps, affectionately referred to as their *Gor Blimey Caps.*

As the weather improved patrols were frequently sent out at night, to the east of Hébuterne across No Man's Land in the direction of Puisieux. Approximately one hundred yards from the German lines, were the Sixteen Poplars leading to the Sunken Road. On 6 March a night patrol had reported German activity with shovels, presumably digging in. During the evening of 1 April a mate of my father Fred Coleman was amongst a small detachment of two officers with twenty five other ranks from "B" Company sent out to engage the enemy. They were in position early, but the enemy were aware of this patrol and sent out a stronger party in excess of fifty men to oppose them.

Several men were injured and fatalities occurred. The task of recovering the injured and dead six hundred yards back to their trenches was hazardous, but carried out with coolness. Fred was wounded whilst helping to recover the casualties. During the time that his wounds were being tended his immediate thoughts were for his comrades as he courageously said, *If there are others worse hit than me go to them; I can stick it.* Fred died of his wounds that evening and was laid to rest in Hébuterne Military Cemetery. In a letter to his parents his Company Commander quoted "Coleman simply gave his life for two of his mates". *Greater love hath no man than this that a man lay down his life for his friends.* (St.John, Chapter 15, Verse 13)

As 1916 progressed plans were formulated for a major offensive, The Battle of the Somme was fought mainly within an area of approximately thirty square miles. From Gommecourt in the north the front line stretched approximately sixteen miles south to Montauban. The 48th South Midland Division then formed part of the 7th Corps within the 4th Army.

Somewhere on The Somme with his mates
My Father: Front Row, Extreme Right

The offensive was planned for 29 June, zero hour fixed for 7.30 a.m. Hundreds of additional Artillery guns were brought forward and positioned behind the British front line. Ultimately fifteen hundred guns of all calibre from light field guns to the mighty howitzers were in position. If spaced evenly along the front it allowed a light field gun every twenty-one yards with a heavy gun every fifty-seven yards.

Mines had been strategically placed along the German front line. Tunnelling companies had previously hewn out soil, rock and chalk to place these huge mines deep under the German lines. Fuses were attached and the tunnels were then back-filled.

During the morning of 24 June an awesome attack was launched as the Artillery guns pounded the German lines relentlessly. Haig was confident that nothing could survive and ultimately it would lead the way for the Infantry to finish the job. Forty-eight hours prior to the planned attack and following heavy rain causing flooded trenches the offensive was postponed until 1 July. During that eight-day onslaught one and a half million shells had been deployed on the enemy lines, but many failed to explode.

Even today after almost one hundred years approximately fifty to sixty tons of unexploded shells are being discovered annually as farmers plough their fields. Aptly referred to as their *iron harvest* they are placed round the perimeter of the fields, to be dealt with later by bomb disposal units.

At 7.20 a.m. on 1 July the Hawthorn Ridge mine was detonated. This was later considered to have been an unwise decision as it alerted the Germans and their Artillery immediately launched a heavy attack on the British trenches. The other mines were detonated at precisely 7.28 a.m. with catastrophic results. The ground heaved and shook, as earth, rock and debris was lifted upwards to a height of 4000 feet. One man braced himself against the rear wall of the trench and one leg stretched firmly against the front trench wall. The shockwaves travelling along the trenches were so violent that his leg shattered below the knee, and was later amputated.

Precisely at 7.30 a.m. the whistles blew signalling the men *over the top,* and although Haig had predicted nothing could have survived he was proved wrong. The men were mown down in their thousands. During the first day of the Battle of The Somme the Allied forces suffered almost sixty thousand casualties; nearly twenty thousand of those were killed. In terms of casualties the 1 July still remains the most costly day in the history of the British Army.

It was a disappointment to the Bucks Battalion that although they had moved forward they did not take part in the first day's offensive. My father must have been one of those who felt that disappointment, although it would not have been realised that the Battle of The Somme would continue for a further one hundred and forty one days.

The Bucks Battalion moved to bivouacs on the Albert-Bapaume road on 17 July for a night reconnaissance of the enemy line between Ovillers and Pozières. The task was delegated to my father's "A" Company and "D" Company. On that occasion they were to ascertain if the Germans were holding four points, and if not they were to be taken. The attacking platoons advanced at 1.00 a.m. but found all to be occupied. The most easterly point was rushed by a platoon from "A" Company. After driving off several bombing attacks they were ordered to withdraw, as the other points had not being taken.

On 19 July the Battalion marched through Albert and took over bivouacs from the Warwicks beside the Albert-Bapaume road. The following day the men were busy drawing all necessary stores. These included Very lights, small arms ammunition, grenades, and shovels all of which would be necessary for their next attack. At 10.30 p.m. Company Commanders gave final orders to the men who advanced to the front line and Sickle Trench approximately two and a half miles distant.

What the men felt during that time leading up to an attack can only be conjectured. They would have received their rum ration, referred to as SRD or "Service Ration Distribution", but cynical interpretations refer to "Soon Runs Dry" or "Seldom Reaches Destination". At the appropriate time the message was passed simultaneously along the line, "Fifteen minutes to go lads". During that short time some men openly prayed that God would give them the strength and courage to do their duty like a man. Many carried a small Bible or New Testament in their breast pocket and possibly referred to a favourite chapter which they read. Others carried photos of wives and family, and kissed them *Good Bye*, just in case. Occasions were recorded when Bibles they carried saved lives taking the sting out of a bullet or shrapnel, that could have proved fatal. When the whistles blew signalling zero hour it was every man for himself as they went over the top into the unknown. Only by personal participation could one ever fully appreciate that experience.

The German line was situated approximately 325 yards from Sickle Trench in the direction of Pozières. The Royal Engineers laid a tape 175 yards from the German line on which the Battalion would form up. Zero hour was fixed for 2.45 a.m. on 21 July. That morning at 2.15 a.m., they left Sickle Trench moving forward to form up on the tape; this was often referred to as *the jumping off point.* The Germans were aware of this move, first sending up flares, then followed this with heavy machine gun fire. As it was not yet 2.45 a.m. the men laid low but were suffering casualties.

At precisely 2.45 a.m. the British guns opened with a roar as thousands of shells flew low over the heads of the Battalion acting as a signal to advance. Such was the onslaught from the German machine-guns that as the men rose they were scythed down. Of those who reached the German lines few returned. That night the Battalion suffered extremely heavy casualties, and the failure of that attack was a bitter blow to the men. They moved back to bivouacs and sleep, but as many of their pals had been lost that would not have been easy.

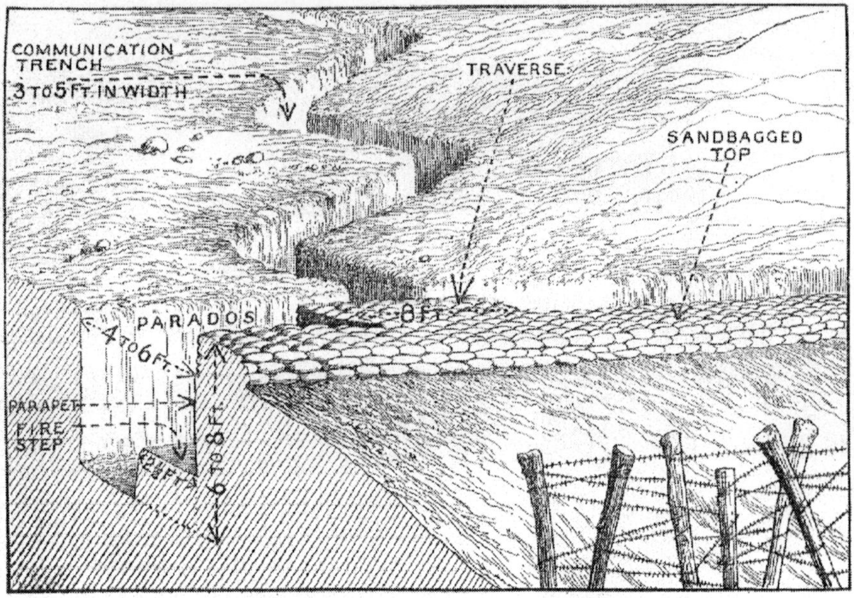


Diagram Showing Typical Front-Line and Communication Trenches

On 22 July the Battalion was in Brigade reserve resting in Mash Valley behind Ovillers. The other three Battalions in the Brigade lined up with the Australians for the night attack on the German positions at Pozières. At 10.00 p.m. the Bucks Battalion left their bivouacs moving forward to support positions. At 00.30 a.m. the guns opened with a deafening roar as the shells screamed through the air towards the German lines. My father's Battalion was brought forward during the night. The Oxford's and Royal Berks, whilst gaining a footing had suffered heavy casualties, but the Gloucesters had been less successful.

The Bucks Battalion was brought forward with orders to attack and seize at all costs the section of the German line that had been attacked by The Gloucesters. This move was to break the German line of defence between Pozières and Thiepval and to pave the way for the eventual capture of Thiepval. Despite suffering extremely heavy casualties that night attack achieved its objective, resulting in the Brigade Commander, Brigadier H. R. Done D.S.O. sending the following communication to the Regimental Commander, Lieutenant-Colonel L.L.C. Reynolds DSO, TD.

*Please give my heartiest congratulations to all ranks of the Regiment under your command, on their gallant and entirely successful attack on July 23. By this success, which was obtained in spite of heavy loss, you enabled the Brigade to carry out the whole of the task allotted, and also make secure the position of the troops who had already gained a footing in the enemy's position on your right.*

A further communication was received,

*The Army Commander wishes to thank all ranks of The 48th Division for their excellent work during the past ten days. By their exertions they have greatly extended our hold on Ovillers and have directly contributed towards the ultimate capture of Pozières.*

Like all Battalions in the 48th Division the First Bucks had suffered heavy casualties during the previous ten days of battle, and new recruits were drafted in. On 26 July the Division moved back and in a series of marches my father's Battalion eventually arrived in Domléger with the prospect of a few days well-earned rest. Their billets there were reasonable, and although training continued they enjoyed some degree of comfort and rest. To reinforce their previous losses a further draft of new recruits were brought in.

Unfortunately time there must have gone far too quickly for the men, and on 9 August my father with his mates started a two-day march back to camp at Bouzincourt, then the target for German shelling. During the early morning of 13 August they moved again through Albert to a line of gun pits west of Usna Redoubt. They were in Brigade reserve then holding the line just west of Pozières. The front line trench was known as Skyline Trench (Sixth Avenue).

A heavy attack that night drove the Oxfords out of Skyline trench. During the afternoon of 14 August the Bucks Battalion moved up with orders to retake this trench relieving the Oxfords now in Ration Trench (Fifth Avenue). Progress throughout the night ensured that by 5.00 a.m. on 15 August all but a short sector of Skyline trench was retaken.

"A" Company then moved back for a few hours rest, whilst "C" and "D" Companies took over the line, with "B" Company in support. During the morning of 15 August the German Army launched a nine-hour continuous bombardment with guns of every calibre on Fifth Avenue and Skyline trench. This shelling and bombing was the heaviest and most prolonged encountered by the Battalion. The men's continued experience in the line enabled them to recognise the approaching shells by the individual noises they made. Shells from lighter guns were known as Minnies up through the range to the heavy artillery referred to as Jack Johnsons. Some shells when exploding left clouds of black smoke, and referred to as coal boxes.

At 11.00 a.m. on 16 August the exhausted Battalion moved back for forty-eight hours rest near to Albert. Shortly after leaving the line they were met by the Divisional General who had his usual cheery word for them. On one occasion when meeting them back from the line he qualified his greeting saying, *Get all the rest you can now, you'll need your arms and legs again tonight.*

There was much to do then such as replacing lost equipment, new drafts being posted in and preparing for action again, allowing little time for rest. Orders were received for an immediate move to the vicinity of Usna Redoubt, where the men bivouacked for the night without blankets. The 143rd Brigade was to attack at dawn and my father and his mates were to be in position to exploit any success. The attack was a complete success and the Battalion moved back to Bouzincourt.

Forty eight hours later they moved forward to Ovillers in support of the 144th Brigade. However, the next day orders were received for an attack by the Battalion during the afternoon of 23 August on the enemy lines between Pozières and Thiepval. "A" and "C" Companies were detailed for the attack, zero hour was fixed for 3.05 p.m.

Key to Map opposite

| | |
|---|---|
| 1. Skyline Trench | 2. Warwick Avenue |
| 3. Sickle Trench | 4.Objective 21 July 1916 |
| 5. Mash Valley | 6. Usna Redoubt |
| 7. Nab Valley (later Blighty Valley) | |

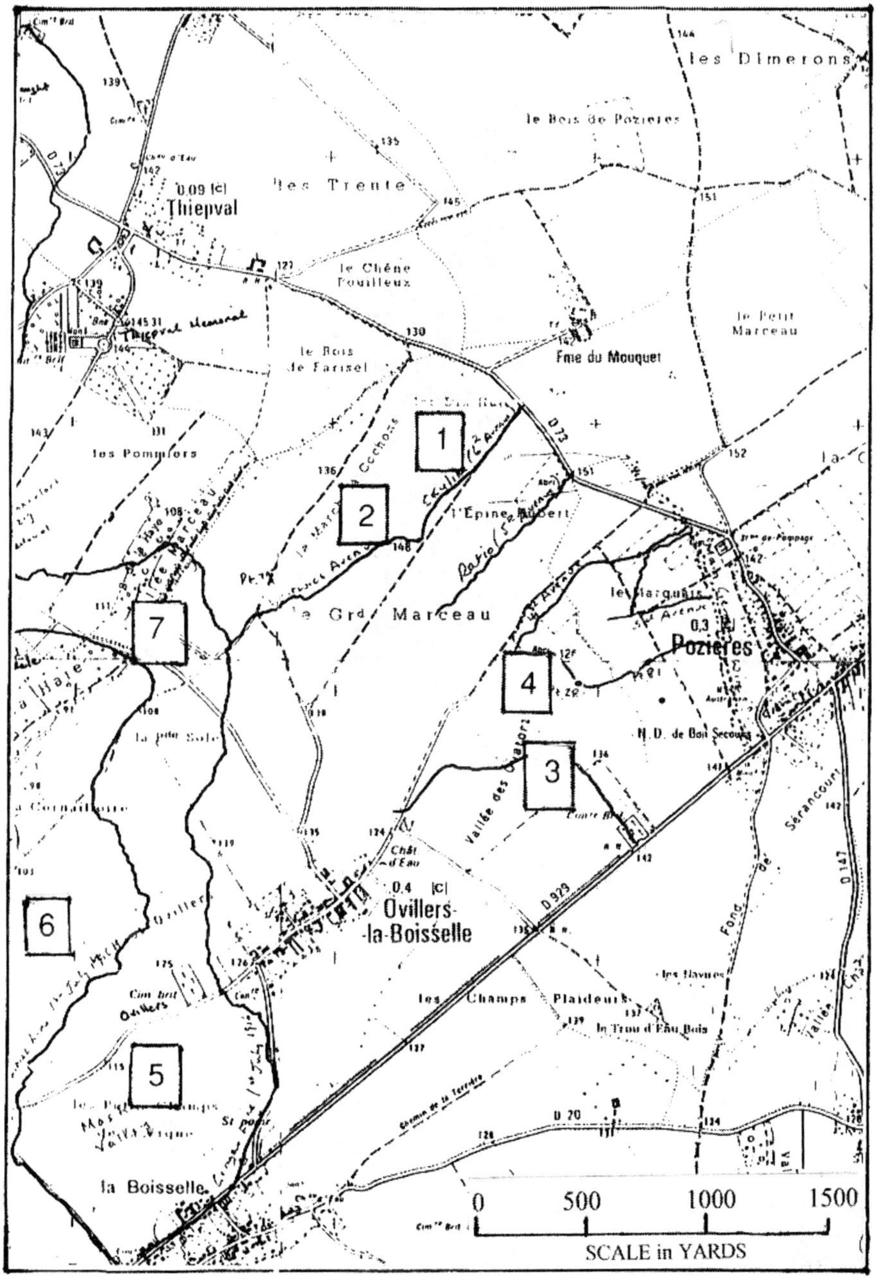
les Dimerons
le Bois de Pozieres
les Trente
0.09 [c]
Thiepval
le Chêne Pouilleux
le Petit Marceau
le Bois de Farisel
Fme du Mouquet
Thiepval Memorial
les Pommiers
1
2
l'Epine Aubert
le Grd Marceau
7
les Margu
Pozières
4
N.D. de Bon Secours
3
Vallée des Chasseurs
Ovillers-la-Boisselle
6
D 929
les Champs Plaideurs
5
la Boisselle
D 73
D 20
D 147
0
500
1000
1500
SCALE in YARDS

The Heavy Artillery carried out a bombardment between 1.00 p.m. and 2.45 p.m. An intense five-minute bombardment then followed at 3.00 p.m. with the field guns providing cover for the infantry attack. Immediately the Battalion came under intense fire from the enemy and suffered heavy casualties rendering progress almost impossible.

Those from the two attacking Companies who survived were now forced to lay out in No Man's land until darkness provided some cover enabling them to return to their trenches. Further casualties resulted during continued attacks by snipers and shellfire. For those lying out they would undoubtedly have appreciated their entrenching tools enabling them to scrape a depression in the ground providing some protection.

Three further nights were spent in the area, with bombing attacks which improved the position. Night patrols were sent out to gain knowledge of the enemy positions, which was handed to the relieving Battalion.

The Somme recorded some of the fiercest fighting during the entire war and some of the men gave accounts of their experiences in their letters home. It was said that at times rifles were of no use when the men charged the enemy lines with fixed bayonets. Memories of the battle for Pozières were described as some of the worst fighting conditions which resulted in carnage. It rained shells and the ground was covered with bodies, and for all of this an Infantryman was paid just one shilling a day.

The Division was finally relieved on 28 August and moved back to Bus-les-Artois. Throughout the previous months fighting on the Somme the Battalion had suffered heavy casualties and became handicapped by insufficient replacements of trained men. Doubtless all Infantry Battalions would have experienced this problem.

The next entry in the Battalion Records for my father states,

*4 September 1916 Granted Class 1 Proficiency Pay*

After spending a week at Bus-le-Artois the Battalion moved to the trenches at Beaumont Hamel. A short time was spent there before moving back to Beauval near Doullens. During a week there further drafts of reinforcements were brought in and training continued. Several more days were spent marching until on 5 October the men were again in Hébuterne.

Rumour spread that an attack was planned on the line at Gommecourt, but this did not materialise. Moving about now from place to place became tiresome, but by early November the men were back defending the front line between Martinpuich and Le Sars. Although that sector was then quieter it was a very inhospitable place. The whole area had been subject to heavy shellfire. The trenches had caved in and were full of water, as was every shell hole. All tracks were deep mud and supplies had to be manhandled over a mile in these conditions. Movement was only possible during the night and extremely hazardous. It was impossible to walk more than twenty yards without falling into a flooded shell hole and becoming covered in mud.

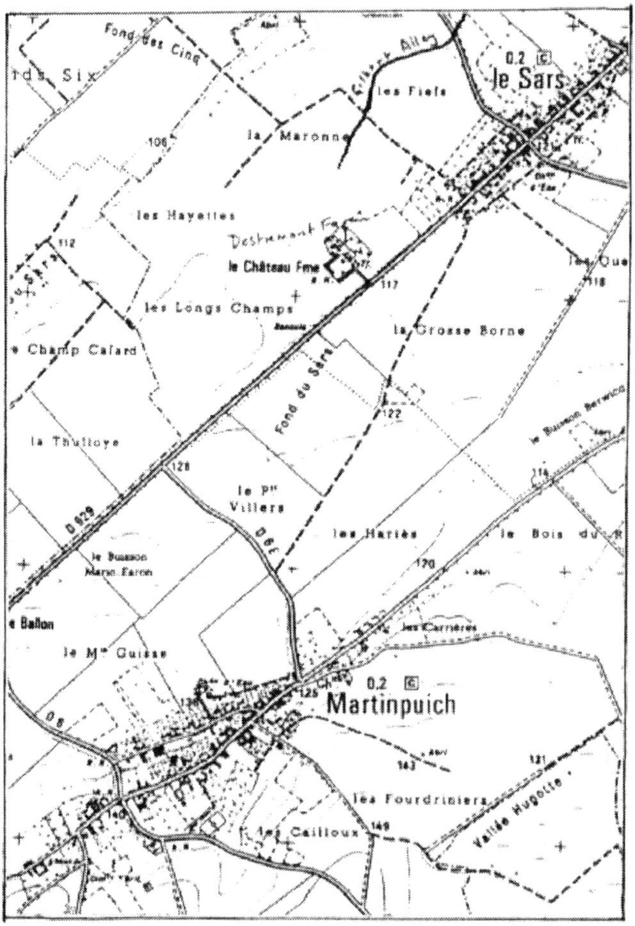

Le Sars had been left uninhabitable and considered of no further importance. Destremont Farm close by had suffered similarly but did contain two large cellars in which two platoons rested each day.

One of the biggest problems faced under such conditions enduring long periods in water and mud was *trench foot.* Whenever possible before going in the front line arrangements were made for my father and his mates to wash their feet, and apply a special solution based on whale oil; efforts were made to issue clean dry socks every twenty-four hours. There were occasions when boots were not removed for several weeks resulting in the skin on their feet peeling off with their socks.

Another problem experienced in the front line trench was boredom. During that time all supplies and food were brought forward from support along communication trenches. In the fire trench the men just waited whilst anticipating the order to attack, or to defend if attacked. During daylight periscopes were used to see across no mans land towards the enemy line. At night patrols were sent out to listening posts. Whatever the weather this was their routine.

During their time in the line three days were spent in the front line, followed by three days in support then three days *at rest,* but the latter was seldom possible.

As Christmas 1916 approached mail order facilities made it possible for family and friends at home to send cigarettes to their loved ones. 1000 Wills Woodbines could be sent at a cost 9 shillings, but Wills Gold Flake, a more luxurious brand cost 15 shillings. These prices included a Christmas card and postage.

The winter of 1916 was exceptionally cold. At Boulogne the sea froze, and life in the trenches must have been appalling. Temperatures plummeted as twenty-five degrees of frost were recorded. The frost was so intense that shaving became a problem as the shaving soap froze to their faces. Water was often in short supply and it became necessary to scoop snow into their mess tins to thaw providing water for washing and shaving. During other occasions when water was unavailable the men saved tea or scooped water from a flooded shell-hole for their daily ablutions. When water was brought to the front it was carried in Jerry cans, previously used for petrol, leaving a lingering taint to all their water, whether for drinking or washing.

My father and his mates in the Battalion must have been feeling the effects of the Somme fighting and in December they were relieved and moved back to Bécourt. Despite poor conditions they enjoyed Christmas dinner of turkey, chestnut stuffing and vegetables. It was three years since my father had enjoyed Christmas with his family and friends at home.

On 17 March 1917 patrols reported back that the enemy trenches opposite were unoccupied. The retirement of the German army from that part of the line had begun.

Chapter Six

## THE HINDEBURG LINE

It would undoubtedly have seemed strange to my father that the German retirement created a degree of *safety* for him and his comrades. That *safety zone* did not last long as on 20 March orders were received for a move to Péronne, approximately fifteen miles to the east of Albert. German shelling had devastated Péronne and much was still burning, presenting a scene of total ruin. As the castle remained reasonably untouched the Battalion headquarters was set up there, whilst the remainder of the Battalion was billeted in cellars around The Square.

A short move forward on 21 March enabled the men to take over an outpost near Doingt. It remained the Divisional line until 26 March. During the evening of the same day there was a further move forward to Tincourt where the men took over billets from the 1/4th Oxfords. Much of this area had been the subject of heavy shelling. At 2.00 a.m. on 5 April the Battalion marched to the railway cutting between Villers-Faucon and St. Emile, acting as reserve to the remainder of the Brigade who were to capture the villages of Lempire, Rossoy and Basse-Boulonge. The attack was a complete success. Prisoners taken revealed that their next outpost ran in front of Tombois Farm and Malakoff Farm.

The Battalion then moved back to Villers-Faucon for the remainder of the day, but took over the line again on 15 April, coinciding with receiving orders of an attack on Tombois Farm. Zero hour was fixed for 11.30 p. m. 16 April. Weather conditions for this night attack across open country could not have been worse. It was pitch black with heavy rain and a gale blowing in the direction of Tombois Farm. These unfavourable conditions led to difficulties when finding the forming–up positions.

A heavy belt of wire hindered their advance, and then at 11.45 p. m. the enemy launched a machine gun attack, accompanied by many flares. To support the Battalion three platoons from the 1/5th Gloucesters were brought in.

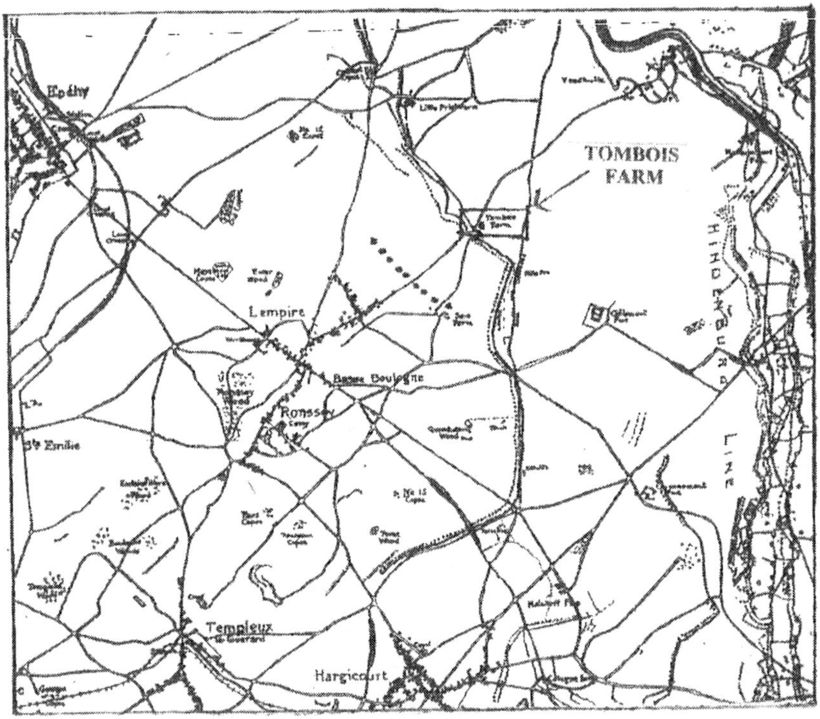


1/1st Bucks attack on Tombois Farm 16/17 April 1917

Forming up positions 11.00 p.m. •••••••••• Zero hour 11.30 p.m.

In their advance "B" Company experienced less wire and consequently was first in the farm, but by 3.00 a.m. both farm and an orchard had been taken. A counter attack along the road was quickly broken up. By daylight on 17 April the Battalion had gained control of several hundred yards of the German trenches either side of the farm. There was no sign of the enemy.

At the end of April the Battalion withdrew from the line marching back to billets at Mons-en-Chassée. This was followed by ten days of strenuous training. Further daily marches started on 11 May as the Battalion returned through the Somme battlefields. Although the British army had laid new roads, the whole area presented a scene of devastation; it was a landscape of shell holes. Villages through which they marched had been totally destroyed.

On 14 May the Battalion took over the line between Hermies and Demicourt, where they frequently experienced artillery fire and bombing. Although they were in this area for several weeks only one engagement was undertaken at midnight on 7/8 June.

The Division was withdrawn from their position on 8 July. Marching west they spent one night in Vélu, followed by a two-day march via Bihucourt, Achiet-le-Grand, Adinfer, and Ransart to Bailleulval. More strenuous training took place as rumours of a major offensive in the Ypres area had been circulating for some time. Suggestions that the Battalion was to be a part of that attack strengthened the necessity for this training. Two additional drafts were brought in bringing the Battalion strength to 25 officers and 920 other ranks.

Chapter Seven

## THE THIRD BATTLE OF YPRES

At 5.00 a.m. on 22 July my father and his mates left Bailleulval marching ten miles south to Mondicourt Station, where they had breakfast. Entraining at 11.30 a.m. they were on their way to The Third Battle of Ypres, frequently referred to as The Passchendaele Offensive. After a seven-hour uncomfortable, weary journey they arrived at Godewaersvelde, (pronounced by the men *God help us,* or, *God wears velvet.)* It was 6.30 p.m. and thoughts that they would spend the night there were quickly dashed, as following tea my father and his mates endured a four hour march north through Watau to scanty billets in tents and barns in Houtkerque. They remained there for seven days.

At midnight on 30/31 July they marched to St. Jans-ter-Biezen just to the east of Poperinge. Shortly after arriving there at 4.00 a.m. the guns of the attacking armies opened with a deafening roar. The Third Battle of Ypres had begun. The weather was unfavourable as towards evening the rain started and continued throughout that night and for the next two days. Word received back from the line was very depressing; the whole area had become a quagmire.

Their advance was postponed as the movement of troops and guns was now impossible. It should be noted here that during the early advance of the German army the Belgian authorities had opened the sluice gates allowing the North Sea to flood much of the Ypres Salient. This was intended to impede the advancing German army but now presented an impediment to the allied army's advance.

On 3 August all Battalion senior officers attended a lecture at Poperinge given by the Corps Commander Lt-General Sir Ivor Maxse. During the next day the Battalion moved forward through Poperinge to Dambre camp, and the support trench. Conditions there were appalling as a sea of mud made movement almost impossible and enemy shelling was continuous. Orderlies and runners faced these conditions to carry important messages and whilst guiding carrying parties.

The Ypres Salient
N
W
E
S
Yser Canal
Steenstraat
Bixschoote
Langemarck
Poelcappelle
Stroombeek
Boesinghe
Pilckem
Passchendaele
Elverdinghe
St. Julien
Gravenstafel
Tyne Cot
Zonnebeke
Wieltje
Frezenberg
St. Jean
Glencorse Wood
Nonne Bosschen
Poperinghe
Vlamertinghe
YPRES
Potijze
Hooge
Polygon Wood
Hellfire Corner
Sanctuary Wood
Polderhoek
Zillebeke
Gheluvelt
Dickebusch
Hill 60
Shrewsbury Forest
Voormezeele
Battle Wood
Kruiseeke
Gheluwe
St. Eloi
Zandvoorde
Mont Rouge
Kemmel
Locre
Mont Kemmel
Wytschaete
Oosttaverne
Ypres-Comines Canal
Menin
Spanbroekmolen
Wervicq
Messines
Wulverghem
Lys
Comines
Warneton
Bailleul
Neuve Eglise
Ploegsteert Wood
Ploegsteert
Lancashire Cottage
Nieppe
Pont de Nieppe
Houplines
Armentières
Lys
Woods
Road
Canals
Rivers
0 1 2 3 4 5 miles

All supplies were brought to the line by pack animals during darkness in knee-deep mud across open country pitted with shell holes. Frequently animals were killed requiring their loads to be transferred to others. The men were obliged to fight and attempt to survive in a sea of glutinous mud.

The Germans had constructed many concrete blockhouses and one captured at Vanheule farm became the Battalion headquarters. Although partly flooded it provided some protection. Cheddar Villa nearby was a more substantial captured blockhouse which became the Regimental aid-post. As it was originally a German blockhouse the entrance faced the retreating Germans, and during the first night there a German shell landed just inside the entrance. One platoon from "D" Company resting inside suffered catastrophic injuries with many dead. After twenty-four hours in the front line and forty eight hours in reserve the Battalion was relieved and moved back to Dambre camp.

Although further rain made the possibility of another attack difficult it was to be resumed as soon as the weather became favourable. On 13 August orders were received for the attack along the whole of the front of the Second and Fifth Armies. The objective for the 145th Brigade would be the high ground overlooking the Stroombeek Valley. Prior to any attack it was vital that relevant details and precise orders were issued. Clause 7 for the attack stated, *The word Retire will not be used, anyone heard to say it will be shot immediately.*

Due to the waterlogged state of the ground the promised tank support unable to get through was cancelled. Despite this lack of support, orders to the Battalions clearly stated *Press on with the attack just the same.*

The strength of "A" Company going into action that night was 3 Officers and 148 O.R's. During the morning of 15 August my father and his comrades left Dambre Camp marching forward as far as the canal bank where they remained for the afternoon. At 9.30 p.m. that evening they moved forward to their forming up positions. The 1/1 st Bucks Battalion formed up with the1/4th Oxfords to their left and the 1/5 th Gloucesters to their right. Zero hour for the attack was fixed for 4.45 a.m.16 August. The Battalion's objective was the area around Triangle Farm approximately 1000 metres north.

That move proved extremely hazardous. It was pitch black and their advance was across ground covered with water filled shell holes during which time the men endured constant heavy shellfire.

Moving forward they crossed the Steenbeek and were in position. What followed was horrendous and described as suicidal. Bayonet charges, hand to hand fighting and a continuous onslaught by the enemy with crossfire resulted in many casualties as men were mown down. It would frequently take at least eight men to stretcher a fallen comrade out of the mud. Many who fell in the shell holes were sucked under and died, as it was impossible to reach them.

By midnight after 19 ¼ hours the conditions they endured had enabled the Battalion to move forward just over half way to their objective. The 1/1st Bucks Battalion casualties during that day were 43 killed, 49 missing and 188 wounded. The survivors were completely exhausted and relieved by the 1/4th Royal Berks, and moved back the following evening to Dambre Camp for *eight days rest*. The Battalion strength was reduced to 16 Officers and 533 O.R's.

On 19 August a communication from the Divisional Commander Major-General Sir Robert Fanshawe to the officer commanding the 145th Brigade included these words,

*It is not the mere capture of positions which is going to bring us the final victory, but the determined fighting, in spite of all difficulties, like that of the First Bucks Battalion, which shows the enemy that he is beaten and cannot hope to beat us and must give in.*

*I have the fullest confidence in your Brigade, and know that they will continue to fight with the same spirit with which they have always done, in spite of difficulties.*

Following their *rest* they moved forward again to the line for further planned operations; the 145th Brigade was to the north-east of St Julien in reserve to the 143rd. and 144th. Brigades. Zero hour for the two attacking Brigades was fixed at 1.55 p.m. on 27 August. The 145th Brigade was then to move forward between the two leading Brigades and capture a line of farms. Heavy rain had again fallen during the previous night, resulting in the battle area being a quagmire. By then the men were used to such appalling conditions, but rifles, bombs and Lewis guns had become caked in mud and unusable. Little gain had been made and the removal of the injured became so hazardous that the task was impossible.

During the following day the 48th Division was withdrawn from the line and moved back. The men hoped they would never see the Ypres Salient again. Their time there must have been indelibly engraved on their minds.

Two weeks were then spent near to St. Jans-ter-Biezen, but during clear nights they suffered German bombing raids. Training was still considered important but this was restricted to mornings, leaving afternoons for some degree of recreation. A further move by train followed on 16 September as the men moved south into northern France detraining at Audruicq north west of St. Omer. A twelve-mile march brought them to Licques, with reasonable billets and more favourable weather, providing a welcome relief.

These more comfortable surroundings were not to last long because at 2.00 a.m. on 27 September the Battalion entrained at Audruicq and returned to the familiar, but inhospitable area of the canal bank close to St Julien.

During the night of 30 September the 1/1st Bucks took over the line from the1/4th Oxfords where an appreciable, although not large gain had been achieved. The farms that had been a previous but unsuccessful target were now in British hands. The Battalions objectives primarily were Tweed House, York and Winchester Farms, then secondly County Crossroads, Vacher Farm and Burns House. Zero hour was fixed for 6.00 a.m. 4 October. Their first objective was gained by 8.30 a.m., and The County Crossroads by 10.30 a.m. Over 300 prisoners were taken as well as anti-tank guns and numerous machine guns. Given further time and favourable weather they were confident that their objectives would have been completed.

On 5 and 6 October it rained continuously. Under those conditions further attacks were impossible, and on the 7 October they withdrew to Dambre Camp. After just two hours preparations to move back to the line were greeted with concern. There was some comfort as a fleet of motor buses took them as far as Wieltje, and from there the men went on foot through St Julien to the line. Heavy rain and shelling did not provide ideal conditions for a successful attack. Zero hour was fixed for 5.20 a.m. on 9 October with the Battalion in Divisional reserve around Cheddar Villa. Considering the appalling conditions endured they had achieved more progress than expected.

During the evening of 10 October the 48th. Division was relieved and left the Ypres battle area for good: Motor lorries provided transport from Wieltje back to Dambre Camp.

On leaving the Ypres sector the Divisional Commander received the following message from General Gough, Commander of the Fifth Army.

*The 48th Division have taken part in much hard fighting during the past two months, including five general engagements. Their spirit and determination on all occasions have been admirable, and temporary setbacks have in no way affected their moral. I am very sorry to bid good-bye to such a dependable Division and feel sure that the future holds many further successes for them.*

What did the future now hold for my father and his mates?

With intolerable weather conditions making further progress totally impossible, the Third Battle of Ypres ended on 11 November and a further major offensive elsewhere was planned.

During the following day Field Marshall Haig's Chief of Staff Lieutenant-General Kiggel was driven to the battle ground area. It was his first visit. When he saw the endless sea of mud and slime overlaid with the torn and twisted debris of war, he broke down and bursting into tears cried

*Good God, Did we really send men to fight in that?* His companion turned to Kiggel and said, *Sir, It gets worse along the road.*

The Battalion spent twenty-four hours at Dambre Camp and forty-eight hours at St. Jans-ter-Biezen. During the evening of 14 October they entrained at Hopoutre heading south through northern France to Ligney-St. Flochiel to the east of St Pol. A long march followed to Mesnil-Bouché where they spent three more days, before moving on to Villers-au-Bois. On 1 November the Battalion went into the line in front of Vimy, which was then reasonably quiet. Rumours suggested that they were to settle there for the winter, but there was speculation that a further move was imminent.

The gravity of the situation in Northern Italy was considered the most likely. At 9.00 a.m. On 14 November the Battalion marched from Le Pendu Camp to billets at Tinques, and given two weeks to refit; Northern Italy was confirmed as their next destination. That move conjured up visions of blue skies and warm sunshine. Transport for the Battalion's move required two trains. During the morning of 23 November all Companies were training, but at 7.30 p.m. "A" and "C" Companies with half the Battalion transport marched from Tinques to Savy to entrain. "B" and "D" Companies with the remaining Battalion transport would leave Tinques twelve hours later.

Chapter eight

## THE ITALIAN FRONT

My father being in “A” company was amongst the first detachment to leave. Their train consisted of one second class coach, two third class coaches, 22 closed trucks, 13 flat bed wagons and two vans. The number of officers in each coach compartment averaged two or three, whilst the men averaged 25 per truck. The train left Savy punctually at 10.38 p.m.

Each truck contained a centrally placed brazier doubling up for cooking and providing some warmth during the cold nights. The next morning the train passed through the Ancre Valley and Albert where survivors of The Somme fighting saw many of their old battlefields. Their journey took them through Amiens, Dijon, and Avignon to the Mediterranean coast at Marseilles. The train then headed east along the French Rivera and Nice. The flat bed wagons not needed for equipment provided sunbathing areas on which the men basked in the warm Mediterranean sunshine. The weather was perfect and local people cheered them on their way; food, oranges, cigarettes, and postcards were thrown to the men, and tea provided at stopping places. Many of the men could not have imagined such scenery existed. My father for example had seldom left his home village. Others stated this was the best holiday they ever had.

The Italian border was crossed at Vintimiglia, where they detrained and enjoyed a march along the sea front. The train then headed north-east to Bologna where Italian deserters were seen chained together. From there heading north, they crossed the river Po, and finally reached their destination. The first train arrived in Bevilacqua at 7.00 p.m. on 29 November; the second train arrived in Este at 8.00 a.m. next morning. It had been a memorable journey of six days and nights.

The following day orders were received of a march to Agugliaro, where the two halves of the Battalion were reunited. During the next four days the combined Battalion experienced long daily marches arriving at Villa del’ Conte on 8 December. A weeks rest there allowed time for washing socks and generally tidying up.

ASIAGO
Roana
Rotzo
Gallio
Foza
Conco
Lusiana
Arsiero
BOLZANO
TRENTO
ROVERETO
RIVA
ARCO
MALCESINE
GARDA
BARDOLINO
LAZISE
SALÒ
GARDONE
DESENZANO
SIRMIONE
PESCHIERA
PADENGHE
Lago di Garda
ORTLES
PRESANELLA
ADAMELLO
DIMARO
CAVALESE
MOENA
AGORDO
SEDICO
BUSCHE
BELLUNO
MAS
BASSANO
MAROSTICA
BREGANZE
SCHIAVON
LUGO
THIENE
PIOVENE ROCCHETTE
SANTORSO
SCHIO
MALO
SOLA VICENTINA
DUEVILLE
CALDOGNO
MOTTA
SANDRIGO
VICENZA
SOVIZZO
ALTAVILLA
TAVERNELLE
MONTECCHIO MAGGIORE
GAMBELLARA
BRENDOLA
LONGARE
MONTEGALDA
GRISIGNANO DI ZOCCO
CITTADELLA
S. GIORGIO IN BOSCO
PIAZZOLA sul BRENTA
LIMENA
CAMPOSAMPIERO
PADOVA
ABANO TERME
PRAGLIA
MONTEGROTTO TERME
BARBARANO
LEGNARO
CAMPONOGARA
STRA
DOLO
MIRA
ORIAGO
MESTRE
VENEZIA
LIDO
NOALE
MIRANO
SCORZÈ
MOGLIANO
PREGANZIOL
TREVISO
CASTELFRANCO VENETO
MONTEBELLUNA
RIESE
ASOLO
ROSA
SAN ZENONE DEGLI EZZELINI
POSSAGNO
CORNUDA
MASER
IL MONTELLO
VALDOBBIADENE
CONEGLIANO
PONTE DELLA PRIULA
PONTE DI PIA
VITTORIO VENETO
SAN PIETRO IN CARIANO
PESCANTINA
PASTRENGO
BUSSOLENGO
SOAVE
S. MARTINO

It was their first opportunity since leaving France, although they were at two hours notice of moving to support the Italian army. On 14 December a further march brought them to S Croce Bigolina, and the Division formed part of X1Xth Corps in reserve to the Italian Army. As an attack there by the enemy was considered a possibility, the Division was to hold a reserve line in the mountains near Rubbio. From there frequent reconnaissances were sent out. Whenever time allowed men attended Church services.

Christmas was approaching and for many, including my father it would be their fourth Christmas away from home and family. Undoubtedly they would be recalling previous family gatherings. With a sense of humour and cynicism Corporal William Baldock compiled his own menu, but on Christmas day the Battalion were able to enjoy turkey and plum pudding, washed down with Italian vino, a more potent wine than that experienced in France, as many were to find out. Twenty-eight days field punishment No 1 resulted for those who were considered to have over indulged.

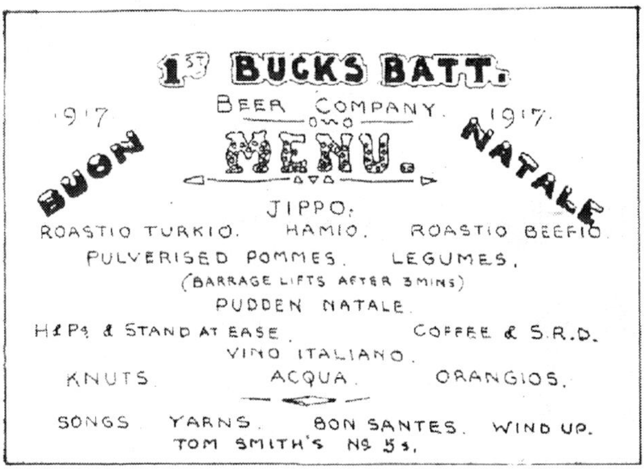
1ST BUCKS BATT.
BEER COMPANY.
1917 1917
BUON NATALE
MENU.
JIPPO.
ROASTIO TURKIO. HAMIO. ROASTIO BEEFIO.
PULVERISED POMMES. LEGUMES.
(BARRAGE LIFTS AFTER 3 MINS)
PUDDEN NATALE.
H&P's & STAND AT EASE. COFFEE & S.R.D.
VINO ITALIANO.
KNUTS. ACQUA. ORANGIOS.
SONGS. YARNS. BON SANTES. WIND UP.
TOM SMITH'S No 5s.

Corporal William Baldock's Christmas Menu

On 24 January 1918 my father and his mates marched daily towards the Piave, but it was a month before they eventually arrived. It was reasonably quiet allowing some time for football, while some officers enjoyed leave in Rome. A further move followed on 14 February to Paese, just west of Treviso. This area had suffered nightly bombing raids from the Austrian and German airmen. On 27 February the Battalion was in support on the Montello followed by a move to the front line along the banks of the Piave River on 3 March. Heavy rain turned the river into a rushing torrent making crossing impossible, and allowing no attack on the enemy.

Rumours spread of a further move and on 14 March the Battalion was relieved by the Italians. Their march west started the next day. They endured a series of long marches during the hot weather, with few rest days. The men finally reached S. Urbano on 3 April. The village lay in the foothills between Vicenza and Verona. The last day had been very strenuous; my father and his mates had marched twenty miles, and without any long halts for meals they were very weary. During that march eighteen men had fallen out and five were taken to hospital. Two weeks were spent there occupied with practise attacks and being equipped for mountain warfare. Officers spent time reconnoitring the line on the Asiago plateau that would be the Battalion's eventual destination. Twenty-five additional pack animals were drafted in although it was feared these would replace their heavy draught horses, but both were retained. The Battalion strength was 40 Officers and 803 O.R's

On the 17 April a move was made to the foothills of the mountain line with overnight halts near Thiene and Mare. Reaching the Asiago plateau involved a steep climb of 2750 feet. On 23 April their ascent to the top followed a slippery mule track hardly recognisable in places. The four and a half-hour climb was accomplished by a ten minute rest after every twenty minute ascent. An infantry man's pack weighed between sixty-six and eighty pounds making climbing very difficult. Although the climb started in warm sunshine during the final few hundred feet the weather became cloudy, cold and wet.

Moving on the Battalion arrived at their camp in Granezza. Water dripped through the roofs of their wooden huts presenting a depressing welcome, and the tracks around were covered with sticky mud. During the morning of the following day the rain turned to snow with thunder and lightning. The snow continued for three days, and was then succeeded by sunshine, interspersed with thunderstorms. Their hopes of warm Italian sunshine were dampened, but as the weather improved the country took on a less desolate appearance. One of the greatest difficulties while in the mountains was maintaining supplies as the divisional ration stores were in the foothills. It was then necessary for rations to be brought half way up the

GRUPPO DI BRENTA
LA MENDOLA
LATEMAR
CATINACCIO
SASSO LUNGO
SELLA
MARMOLADA
SASS SONGHER
PALE DI SAN MARTINO
CIMA PORTULE
2308
CIMA DODICI
CIMA UNDICI
2228
M. ORTIGARA
2106
CIMA DELLA CALDIERA
2124
LOZZE
CORNO DI CAMPO VERDE
2129
CORNO DI CAMPO BIANCO
CIMA MANDERIOLO
CIMA LARICI
M. VERENA
2019
M. ZEBIO
M. CIMON
1768
M. MELETTA DI GALLIO
M. FIOR
1824
MELETTE DI FOZA
ROTZO
943
ROANA
1000
CAMPOROVERE
1057
ASIAGO
1001
GALLIO
1093
FOZA
1083
COSTALTA
SISEMOL
CANOVE
1001
ALBAREDO
TOCCO
MEZZASELVA
CONCA
1097
MOSCA
913
M. TORLE
CAVALETTO
CONCO
830
LUSIANA
752
RUBBIO
COGOLLO DEL CENGIO
CHIUPPANO
SASSO ROSSO
VALSTAGNA

mountain; then transported to the top by horses which found the ascent demanding. Eventually army lorries were used to take up the rations.

During early May the weather improved with hot sunny days, but were then were followed by further heavy rain on 13 May, and continuing for several days. Little happened during this first tour in the mountains, but on 19 May the Battalion started their move back down to the plains where the heat was intense. On 21 May they paraded at 4.50 a.m. and marched 6 miles to camp at Rovere. Marches were then carried out during the night avoiding the heat of the day. Leaving at 9.40 p.m. that same day they marched to Grumo and Cereda arriving at 5.00 a.m. the following morning. As daytime temperatures soared into the 80's and 90's Khaki light drill replaced their heavy serge clothing, and with the issue of pith helmets the heat became marginally more bearable.

My Father

During the intense heat training was undertaken during the cool early mornings and evenings, but at all other times the men lay and gasped in the heat.

A typical day's timetable became,

| | |
|---|---|
| Reveille | 5.00 a.m. |
| Breakfast | 5.30 a.m. |
| Training | 6.30 a.m. - 10.30 a.m. |
| Teas | 11.00 a.m. |
| Dinners | 3.30 p.m. |

Training continued during the evenings.

It was expected that the Battalion would remain in the plains for three weeks, when suddenly orders were received to relieve the 7th Division who were holding the line. Following two long early morning marches the men were again back at the foot of the mountain at Camisino, but at 4.30 a.m. on 1 June the Battalion negotiated a 3,000 feet climb up a rough steep mule track in five hours. Despite that early start the heat during the last hour proved extremely tiring.

The 48th Division's line now extended to approximately 4,500 yards, but the actual trench line was nearer to 6,000 yards. The Battalion's sector lay on the extreme right of the Divisional line about 700 yards south of Roncalto and at a point where they joined the 23rd. Division's line. It then stretched west to Gelpac Fork. Their front lay well inside the woods, whilst the enemy front line trenches were in the open about 1,400 yards distant. Coinciding with this move the Battalion suffered from an acute bout of influenza, some men were affected more than others, and a few sent to hospital.

During the nights the enemy pushed out into No Man's Land, eventually occupying Vaister Farm considered as a possible inconvenience to the Battalion during an expected forthcoming offensive. It was decided to attack Vaister during the night of 8/9 June. Several attacks and counter attacks followed with the final eviction of the enemy.

Plans were then formulated for a combined offensive with the French Army to drive the enemy off the plateau back to their original line about one and a half miles behind their present positions. If successful it would give the advantage of being nearer to holding Mount Catz, Mount Interrotto and the mountains overlooking the Val d' Assa. However the Battalion was relieved in the line and moved back into Brigade support. During the evening of 14 June commanding officers were warned of a possible attack by the enemy the following morning, but plans for their own attack on 16 June were to continue.

At 3.00 a.m. on 15 June the Austrian guns of every calibre opened with a roar on all lines of the British front. A considerable number of gas shells were also used. Ammunition dumps were hit, creating the domino effect and trees crashed to the ground all around. The Bucks Battalion immediately occupied its positions in Lemerle Switch Trench and Polderhoek Trench. Orders were received to hold these positions until the last man. This enemy onslaught continued for several hours with considerable accuracy.

The enemy's infantry attack commenced at 7.00 a.m. as they infiltrated into the wood, but it was extremely difficult to see their advance, and a thick ground mist presented further complications. Throughout the day fierce fighting prevailed, with attacks and counter attacks resulting in losses and gains. During that onslaught Albert Kent (my father's cousin) 1/4th Oxfords was killed in action. Albert was laid to rest close to where he fell in the secluded Boscon Cemetery

Plans were formulated for a counter-attack to take place at 4.30 a.m. on 16 June. There was very little resistance and by 5.45 a.m. the original front line had been retaken. A message found on the body of a dead Austrian officer gave details of a pending withdrawal to be implemented at 2.50 a.m. back to their original lines. The weight of numbers of the enemy had enabled them to get this far, but possibly their lack of push and enterprise prevented them from exploiting their break through further. During this engagement the enemy suffered heavy casualties, as became evident across the recaptured battlefield area.

The following day was taken up with the men repairing the wire barricades, burying the dead and clearing the battlefield. There appeared to be a certain amount of complacency amongst the enemy, and their moral seemed shaken. On 18 June the men had baths whilst the remainder of the day was spent with inspections and generally clearing up.

On 20 June Major General Sir Robert Fanshawe relinquished command of the Division. After three years he had earned the respect of everyone who had served under his command. During that time he became known as the chocolate soldier. In his satchel he had carried small chocolate bars that he freely gave to those he met; frequently he had been the first to meet the men returning from the line. Major General Sir H B Walker succeeded him.

During the following day all Companies had box respirators inspected by the Divisional Gas Officer.

The145th Brigade moved back from the line on 30 June and a series of marches returned to Granezza, but with frequent successful night raids on the enemy line.

On 4 August "B", "C" and "D" Companies attended a special Church parade to commemorate the 4th anniversary of the declaration of war. "A" Company provided a working party.

During 8 and 9 August successful raids were carried out on the enemy trenches along almost the entire British and French fronts. Further attacks followed between the British line and Asiago, signalling a turning point in the war. The Austro-Hungarian forces were suffering heavy casualties and hundreds of prisoners taken.

During September entries for my father appearing in The Battalion War records state

*Granted 7 days leave to Sirmionne 11-9-18 to 17-9-18.*

Sirmionne situated on the southern shore of Lake Garda must have seemed like paradise for my father as he was away from the guns and the front line, now with some of his mates they could briefly relax.

A further entry on 29-9-18 states

*Deprived 6 days pay for being in a trench out of bounds.*

It is my belief that his reason for being in that trench was going in search for news of his cousin Albert Kent. My father may only just have received news that Albert had been killed during the Battle of Asiago on 15 June.

Towards the end of September the 48th Division was the only British Division holding the line. Although there were plans to send the 7th and 23rd Divisions back to France, the situation changed and they remained in Italy.

At about the same time all Brigades in the British Force serving in Italy were reduced to three Battalions. From the 145th Brigade the 1/5th Gloucesters were withdrawn and returned to France.

During early October the British Commander in Chief was in command of the combined Italian-British armies with possible operations on the Piave. During the night of 28/29 October the Bucks Battalion carried out a raid in the area Sec, S M. Maddalena and Cassordar expecting to beat all previous records in numbers of prisoners taken. To their dismay the enemy had evacuated the whole area and withdrawn 3,000 yards to the rear at the foot of the mountains. One Austrian had remained behind to let off Verey lights. It was certainly no record to take just one prisoner. Asiago was in British hands and the time was right to deliver a final decisive blow. A brief telephone message conveyed the orders to achieve this result

The 48th Division central between the 24th French Division and the 20th Italian Division was detailed to attack and capture the line between Croce di S. Antonio and Mount Mosciagh. The attack was to start at 5.45 p. m. on 1 November. My father and his mates in the First Bucks Battalion formed up on the line between Rendela and Ferragh; their final objective was a line of approximately 800 yards due east of Croce di S. Antonio. The area across which they were to advance lay in the mountains.

At the time these orders were received the Battalion was in rest huts north of the Kaberala road. It was 1.00 a.m. and the majority of the men were asleep. Zero hour was fixed at 5.50 a.m. Time was crucial if they were to reach their forming-up point about seven miles away. Companies were to wear fighting order, water bottles must be filled and haversack rations were issued. Packs and blankets were to be left in the vacated huts; carrying parties remained to arrange their removal. Attempts were made to provide tea for the men prior to leaving, but the majority had to leave without.

The men hoped for favourable conditions to ensure they reached their attacking positions. Their route took them across the old No Mans Land and through Asiago, but fortunately the road had been reasonably well repaired. When reaching the northern outskirts of Asiago enemy shelling was experienced and progress became more difficult. It was 5.30 a.m. when they arrived at the forming-up positions. Although some resistance was experienced by 7.00 a.m. Mount Catz was taken. Now on top of the mountain they were spotted and came under attack from enemy shelling. There was no time to hang around; they had to get on with the job.

Their advance proceeded with little opposition. It appeared that the enemy was beaten. Some isolated pockets of resistance proved of little danger and the enemy quickly surrendered. The Battalion was on the move and in sight of victory. By 10.30 a.m. they reached a line at approximately the 4,600 feet contour, south-west of Croce di S. Antonio, but were now out of touch with the French and Royal Berks.

It had been known for some months that the enemy had gun positions in the Valle di Nos so reconnoitring parties were sent out to investigate. Many guns were found; some of these had obviously been firing until the ammunition ran out. Others were used until the last minute; their breechblocks were removed and then abandoned. During the day hundreds of prisoners were taken, together with various guns and other equipment. It appeared the enemy had lost the will to fight.

It was mid-day and the Battalion remained in position during the rest of that day and night. Following a long eleven hours on the move the men were tired and the lack of a cup of tea did nothing to relieve the situation. The Battalion was on the top of a mountain in the middle of a wood. As their rations had not arrived, guides were sent out to find the transport column but the darkness in an unknown wood containing various mule tracks made finding it impossible. By the time the rations had been found and brought forward the Battalion had moved again. This was the second day they had been forced to set off without even a cup of tea and this time they were without water and rations.

At 7.00 a.m. the following morning the First Bucks moved off heading west. They first scaled Mount. Dorbelle and then Mount. Mosciagh where they relieved the 7th Worcestershire Battalion. It was not until 2.00 p.m. that their rations and water finally arrived. It was necessary to be careful with these supplies as their rate of progress in an unknown direction meant it could have been some time before further supplies arrived. On top of Mount. Mosciagh the retreating enemy had abandoned guns of all calibre, stores and equipment, clear evidence of a hasty retreat.

During mid afternoon orders were received by the Battalion to move down into the Vaille di Portule, and rejoin the Brigade where they had bivouacked for the night. Although they found some enemy huts there they contained insufficient room for shelter. Consequently many were forced to spend a freezing night in the open with neither greatcoats nor blankets to provide any warmth. The huts contained stoves providing limited heat and the retreating enemy had left much of their equipment together with books and magazines strewn around. There was a general state of filth and abandoned clothing was infested with vermin. However a well-stocked food store was promptly raided.

At 3.00 a.m. on 3 November the Division resumed its forward march. At 4.30 a.m. the 143rd. Brigade attacked the Vezzena position but despite being aware of the strength of the enemy in this position, little resistance was offered. By 8.00 a.m. fourteen enemy Battalions were surrounded and captured. Amongst these were the 3rd Austrian Corps Commander, Divisional Commanders and their staff. Their huts contained substantial food although it seemed the Austrian army did not appreciate it as the men were looking under nourished.

The Division's advance towards Vezzena now headed by .The First Bucks proved memorable. In the enemy's hurry to leave they had abandoned guns and wagon parks, and ammunition dumps lay along the route. In order to leave as lightly as possible they had left gas masks, helmets, packs, haversacks and even rifles scattered along the route. This picture of desperate abandonment must surely have been seen as the enemy's total lack of moral and knowledge that their war was over. They were a defeated army.

Moving nearer to Vezzena more Battalions of the enemy were seen under the escort of a few British soldiers, and some were led by one Austrian carrying a white flag. As they approached Vezzena after seven hours on the road the Battalion was probably feeling the effect of hunger and stopped for a meal.

Along the road between Vezzena and Mount. Rovere a group of about 500-600 enemy were seen, all were carrying rifles but they were reluctant to use them. Their officer in charge was ordered forward and instructed to order his Battalion to march past and lay down its guns. There was no resistance to this order.

Moving on down the steep slopes of Mount. Rovere the Division marched into the Val Sugana, and by 3.30 p.m. occupied Caldonazzo. During that afternoon officers proceeded to The Third Austro-Hungarian Army's headquarters in Trent, demanding the surrender of Trent and Pergine and all hostile troops. They complied with this demand.

The same night the 144th and 145th Brigades were billeted in Caldonazzo, but with 10,000 prisoners to guard there was little sleep for the men. After a very long exhausting day "A" and "B" Companies spent four hours during that night providing guard duty for the prisoners. The Division had 22,000 prisoners to control. There was a certain amount of hostility amongst the different nationalities, some spat in each others faces. Others refused to stretcher the wounded of another nationality, until they were shown the business end of a bayonet. The Battalion strength was 26 Officers and 632 other ranks.

During that day the Battalion had been on the move for fourteen hours and covered twenty-five miles across a difficult terrain, mopping up thousands of prisoners on its way. For some time the men had had little sleep and were often short of water and supplies. Many men were probably wondering how much longer they could continue without rest and food.

At approximately 7.00 a.m. on 4 November the news they had so patiently and so deservedly earned was received:

*Armistice with Austria-Hungary has been signed 3rd November. Armistice will come into effect from 15.00 hours 4th November. Moves ordered for 4th. November will take place, but all troops will halt on the line gained at 15.00 hours exactly. All Austrians within the line gained this hour will be considered prisoners-of-war. Austrians not within this line will at 15.00 hours retire for a distance of at least three kilometres. The utmost care will be taken to see that these instructions are carried out. The contents of this wire will be immediately passed to all units who are in touch, in case they should not receive them by other methods. Acknowledge.*

The Battalion first received this news quietly; they were exhausted and far too weary to be jubilant; once again their rations had not arrived. That was a situation which by then the men were becoming accustomed, and never a time for celebrations, but the efforts of Quartermaster finally ensured their delivery.

Since 1 November the Division had taken 22,000 prisoners, captured 165 Howitzers, 263 other guns plus uncountable small arms, machine guns and other equipment. Countless numbers of abandoned guns still lay in the region of Vezzena along the Val d'Assa.

That peace would undoubtedly have been an unforgettable experience for my father and his comrades. The guns fell silent and the birds would have been heard singing again. During a conversation with one veteran he described that abrupt silence as an eerie experience.

The1/4th Oxfords remained in charge of prisoners, the remainder of the Brigade left at 10.00 a. m. A sixteen mile march brought them to the small village of Madrano to the east of Pergine. During this march the men witnessed pitiful sights. Towns and villages were filthy. Dead horses lay along the roadside from which famished locals were cutting rump steaks.

During the evening of 4 November the Divisional Commander issued the following order of the day:

*OFFICERS, NCOs and MEN of the 48th DIVISION,*

*Your achievements during the last few days of the most profound military events deserves unstinted praise. After fourteen weeks of trench warfare and arduous work, chiefly at night, combined with frequent raids of the most difficult though successful nature, you have undertaken an attack on a front originally allotted to two Divisions, against what ought to have been impregnable mountain positions; you have swept away the enemy rearguards, and acting as the vanguard of the Sixth Italian Army, you have advanced so rapidly and with such resolution, that the retiring enemy have had no time to reform and have left over 20,000 prisoners, hundreds of guns and immeasurable booty in the hands of the Division.*

*The mere performance of the march in the time, and under the conditions you endured, would have been, even without opposition, considered a creditable feat. You can justly claim that the favourable situation of the Italian Armies on this front at 15.00 hours today when one of the most memorable armistices in history was signed, is largely due to your exertions and resolution.*

*As your Divisional Commander I cordially thank you.*

*(Sd.) H. B. Walker, Major General, Cdg. 48 th. Division.*

News received from The Western Front revealed that the war there was proceeding satisfactory, but there remained the possibility that the Battalion might return there again. My father and his mates anticipated that the war for them was over. On 6 November orders were received of a return to Caldonazza. They left next morning for the six day march of eighty miles. One overnight stop at Val Portule was described as crowded accommodation in huts containing an ample supply of fleas. Before starting this march the men had acquired a collection of wagons and horses. Austrian dumps provided them with supplies, and it was decided to load the wagons with flour, oats and hay.

Each man was issued with sufficient flour to make his own pudding. However one man thought that stolen flour, like stolen kisses, would be the sweetest; he broke into the wrong hut and was later seen trying to make his pudding from cement. On 11 November the Battalion paraded at 7.30 a.m. and marching through Val D'Assa, Camporovere and Asiago arrived back in their old haunts in Granezza.

At 3.00 p.m. on 11 November whilst in Granezza the Battalion received the news that an Armistice had been signed with Germany.

*THE GREAT WAR WAS FINALLY OVER.*

Initially there was little excitement at receiving the news. For those fortunate enough to have survived their thoughts were for their comrades who would not return to rebuild a life back home.

However they realised this was the news they had been waiting for. During the previous ten days the men had endured strenuous marches and fighting whilst completely overwhelming the Austrio-Hungarian army. They were proud to be a part of that great victory.

My father and his mates then faced a twenty-two mile march down to Thiene where they handed over all their captured wagons and supplies to the Italian authorities. During the next day and after a march of eighteen miles they arrived in the villages of Maglio and Novale. It was assumed the billets there would be their last, and every man was surely convinced that he would be amongst the first to be released.

Discipline in spite of the war's end when it could have been more relaxed became stricter; *spit and polish* was the order of the day. Inspections by the Divisional, Brigade, and a French Divisional Commander were followed by congratulations to the Battalion. After a few weeks it was said the Battalion was looking smarter than at any time since leaving Chelmsford on 30 March 1915.

Training continued but this still left time for the men to enjoy competitive sport. The Battalion was proud in achieving their share of the honours. During the morning of 29 November the Battalion enjoyed another route march, but during the afternoon "A" Company lost by Two goals to Nil to "B" Company in the Brigade football competition.

On 8 December the Battalion paraded at 10.15 a.m. for a memorial service for the Officers N.C.O's and men who had fallen during the war.

Undoubtedly that service would have brought back many memories of their comrades with whom they had served.

Another Christmas was spent away from home. My father and his pals would surely have thought of their missing pals, tingeing the celebration with sadness. For my father it was his fifth Christmas parted from his family and friends in Aston Abbotts.

During the previous four years it had been possible to secure turkeys for the Battalion's Christmas dinner, but in 1918 they had acquired several live pigs. A "pig board" was appointed to ensure their welfare and that they enjoyed their last days before becoming Christmas dinner for a hungry Battalion. All Companies had sufficient tables and forms ensuring everyone sat down for Christmas dinner. "Home-fed" pig was much more popular than turkey, and the 1918 Christmas dinner of roast pork, vegetables, plum pudding, oranges, nuts and beer was voted a huge success.

The Battalion strength then was 19 Officers and 613 other ranks. On 29 December teams of thirty men competed to represent their Battalions in the Brigade cross country race over a distance of 3½ miles. The 1/1st Bucks were more successful than in football gaining first place within the Brigade.

The men's thoughts then concentrated on returning to England with a final parade and dismissal in the Market Square, Aylesbury; they were so proud of their achievements. However the Battalion was gradually broken up in Italy. Demobilisation initially started slowly but increased during January and February 1919 with upwards of fifty men each week returning home to England. A cadre party of five officers and fifty men remained in Italy to ensure the return of the Regimental stores.

The Battalion records for my father states,

*Transferred to England for dispersal (Purfleet) 7-2-19*

After 4½ years service during The Great War my father was finally demobilised on 9 March 1919 and returned home to rebuild his life, a life that had been interrupted by war, and turned upside down. Undoubtedly his thoughts and memories would have frequently returned to the battlefields whilst remembering his mates who would not be returning home, many still lay buried where they fell, with no known grave. It would have been impossible to erase those experiences from his memory.

Oxf Bucks L.I.
2883

CERTIFICATE of* Discharge / ~~Transfer to Reserve~~ / Disembodiment / ~~Demobilization~~ on Demobilization.

Army Form Z. 21.

Regtl. No. 265662 Rank Private

Names in full Kent George Sydney
(Surname first)

Unit and Regiment or Corps from which *~~Discharged~~ ~~Transferred to Reserve~~ 1/1 Bucks. Oxf-Bucks Light Inf

Enlisted on the 4th September 1914

For Oxf - Bucks Light Infantry
(Here state Regiment or Corps to which first appointed)

Also served in

Only Regiments or Corps in which the Soldier served since August 4th, 1914 are to be stated. If inapplicable, this space is to be ruled through in ink and initialled.

Medals and Decorations awarded during present engagement: Authorised Prior to 11th November 1918 / Nil / Nil

*Has / ~~Has not~~ served Overseas on Active Service.

Place of Rejoining in case of emergency Chiseldon Medical Category A

Specialist Military qualifications Nil Year of birth 1894

He is* ~~Discharged~~ / ~~Transferred to Army Reserve~~ / Disembodied / ~~Demobilized~~ on 8th March 1919.

in consequence of Demobilization.

Signature and Rank.

Officer i/c Infantry Records. Warwick (Place).

* Strike out whichever is inapplicable. † The word "Nil" to be inserted when necessary.

(20996). Wt. W 8211—P.P. 2329. 8,000m. 1/19. D & S. (E 1256.)

N.B.—Any person finding this Certificate is requested to forward it in an unstamped envelope to the Secretary, War Office, London, S.W. 1.

WARNING.—If this Certificate is lost a duplicate cannot be issued. You should therefore on no account part with it or forward it by post when applying for a situation.

I have often wondered how much, or indeed how little he would have told my late brother and me about the horrors he experienced of serving in the front line and trenches.

MY FATHER'S ARMY REFERENCE

Issued in January 1919 by the Officer commanding the 48th. Division

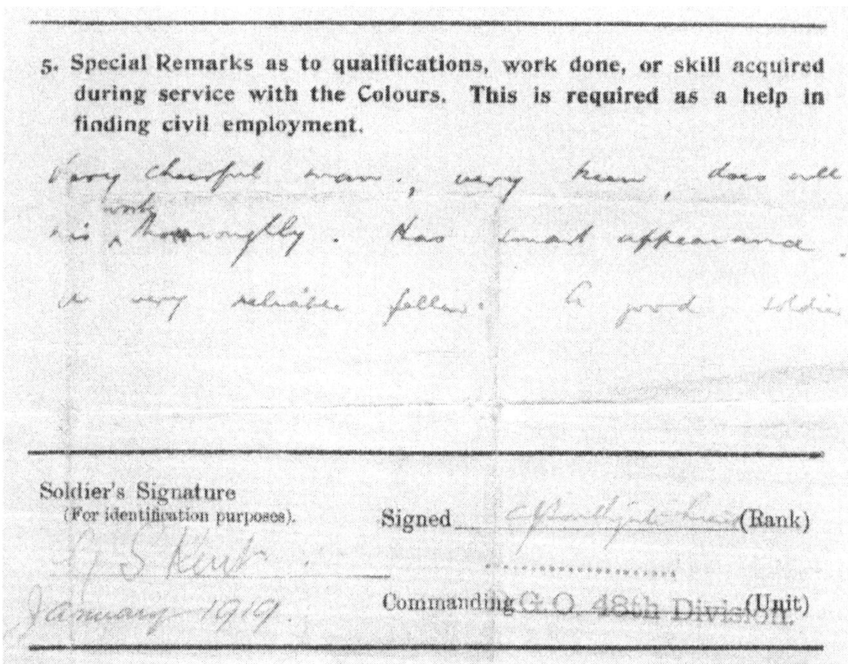

5. **Special Remarks as to qualifications, work done, or skill acquired during service with the Colours. This is required as a help in finding civil employment.**

Very cheerful man, very keen, does all his work thoroughly. Has smart appearance. A very reliable fellow. A good soldier.

Soldier's Signature
(For identification purposes).

Signed [illegible] (Rank)

Commanding G.O. 48th Division (Unit)

January 1919.

*Very cheerful man, very keen, does all his work thoroughly,*
*Has smart appearance, A very reliable fellow, A good soldier*

*NO ONE CAN ASK FOR MORE THAN THAT*

FOR KING & COUNTRY

# ROLL OF HONOUR

THE PRIMITIVE METHODIST CHURCH & SUNDAY SCHOOL ASTON-ABBOTTS

| | | |
|---|---|---|
| G. KENT. | 1st. Batt. Bucks Territorials. | |
| F. HALSEY. | " " " " | |
| ALBERT ELLIS. | " " " " | |
| J. ELLIS. | Royal Bucks Hussars | |
| C. SIMMONS. | " " " | |
| S. SMITH. | 2nd. Batt. Bucks Territorials. | |
| A. BATES. | " " " " | |
| ARTHUR ELLIS. | Canadian. | |
| A. KENT. | 3rd. Batt Bucks Territorials. | Died in Italy. June 15th. 1918. |
| E. SMITH. | " " " " | |
| S. JEFFS. | " " " " | Died in France. July 24th. 1916. |
| J. HIGGS. | A.S.C. Mechanical Transport. | Died on return from Active Service. |
| C. ELLIS. | A.S.C. | |
| W. SMITH | O. & B.L.I. | Died in France. Sept. 20th. 1917. |
| G. HUMPHREY. | R.Es. | |
| H. SIMMONS. | A.S.C. | |
| W. FLEET. | O. & B.L.I. | |
| W. PARKER. | " | |
| J. SIMMONS. | Canadian. | |
| A. BRAZIER. | R.F.A. | |
| W. BURROWS. | Cycling Corps. | |
| W. BIERTON. | Training Reserve. | |
| P. BRAZIER. | Queens Own Oxford. Hussars. | |
| A. JEFFS. | R.G.A. | |
| H. KENT. | 51st. Batt. Devonshire Regt. | |

GOD SAVE THE KING

A Collection from My Father's Memorabilia

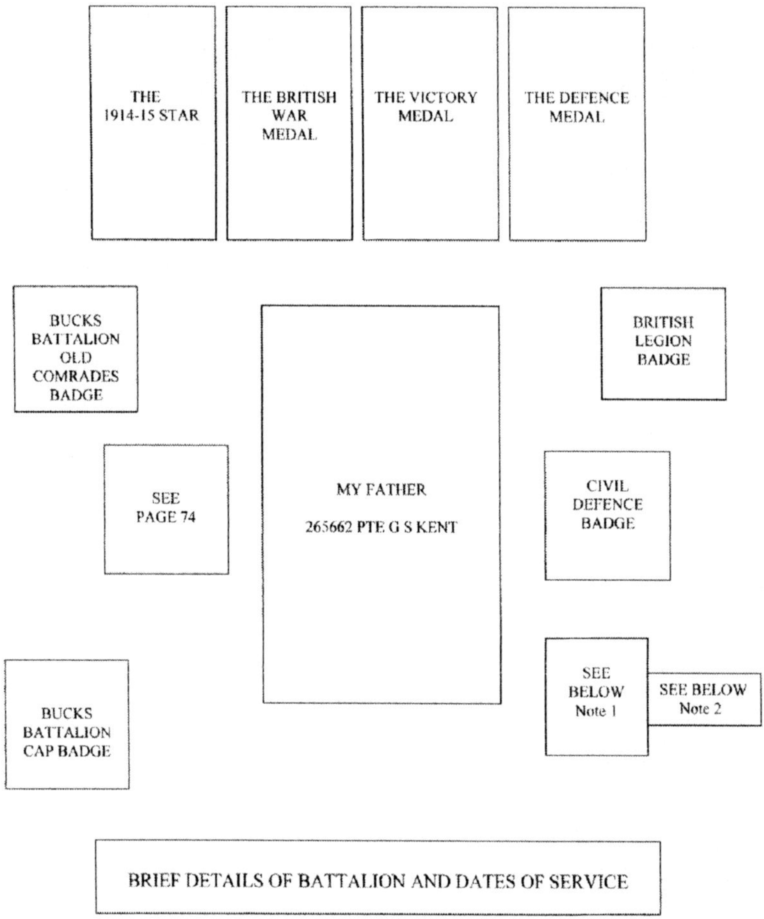


Note1. Brave Conduct Badge awarded to my father, acknowledging his leading roll in rescuing the pilot from a crashed and burning plane near to his place of work 18 September 1942.

Note 2.H M King George V1 acknowledged my father's brave conduct and recommended the award of The Silver Laurel Leaf.

Chapter Nine

# A PILGRIMAGE TO THE FRONT

Although always aware that my research could never be complete, I planned to visit some of the battlefield areas where my father served, to help me gain a deeper understanding of the war he knew. I realised that there would now be little evidence of trenches. The vast area of The Western Front that meandered 460miles from the Belgian coast to the borders between France and Switzerland would have been reclaimed and reverted to its original use.

However, from anywhere on The Somme, within The Ypres Salient or The Asiago Plateau it is impossible to be far from one of the hundreds of cemeteries, where so many men who fell in The Great War now lie buried. These cemeteries so immaculately maintained by The Commonwealth War Graves Commission present a stark but poignant reminder of the sacrifice made by our forebears. The visitor to any of these areas will be aware that thousands of courageous young men, who paid the ultimate sacrifice, still lie buried where they fell. They have no known grave. I felt compelled to make a pilgrimage to the Western Front and the Italian Front.

During the latter part of 2000 I started planning my first visit to The Somme and Ypres which became a reality during September of the following year. I had previously read a journalist's article featuring a guesthouse in Auchonvillers (pronounced by the British Tommy as Ocean Villas) ideally situated on The Western Front and approximately six miles north of Albert. The location appeared to provide everything for those researching a family connection with The Great War.

The guesthouse is owned by Avril Williams. Shortly after moving to France to start a new life Avril purchased a derelict farmhouse on 1st July 1992 but with no clear plan what to do with it. Her first thoughts were to convert the barn into gites, but the subsequent discovery of a cellar beneath her farmhouse revealed graffiti connected to The Great War. It had been a Dressing Station helping to treat the endless numbers of casualties resulting from the Battle of The Somme. Avril felt she had to preserve that important part of history. Jack Horsfall was the first historian to share Avril's view and offered valuable encouragement during times she felt unable to continue.

Having decided to meet the needs of people coming in search of their loved ones graves Avril started a tea-room in her living room to attract her next years B&B visitors. As soon as the first bedroom was ready it was let and by 1993 she had three bedrooms and a small tearoom. More bedrooms were opened to welcome the increasing numbers of visitors, and the large tearoom catering for the increasing number of visitors is now located in the adjoining barn.

With my wife Jean we left Dover on the early ferry 4 September 2001 arriving in Calais at 9.00 a.m. We drove south-east on the A26 motorway to Lillers, then south through St Pol to Doullens. This latter road runs parallel with, and close to the railway that on 18 July 1915 my father and his mates travelled from Berguette to Doullens and The Somme. From Doullens we followed as closely as possible their route to Hébuterne. But whilst they were on foot we enjoyed the comfort of our car.

I had reserved our accommodation at Avril's guesthouse; it was lunchtime when we arrived to a warm welcome. Whilst enjoying home made soup, fresh crusty bead and a pot of tea with Avril it was soon evident there was a relaxed atmosphere with few house rules.

As there was little time to explore far from the guesthouse that afternoon we decided to visit the Newfoundland Memorial Park just a very short drive near Beaumont-Hamel. I was already aware of the preserved battlefield there but this first visit was of particular interest to me as my father had seen action there on two, albeit, short occasions during his two years on The Somme.

Inside the Memorial Park was an excellent visitor and information centre that guides the visitor as it graphically explains the war in this area. After a short walk we were at the British Front line trenches. My thoughts immediately turned to my father. Was I sharing the same view he had seen eighty-five years earlier? I looked down the hill across No Man's Land pitted with shell holes to the German trenches about two hundred yards distant. Naturally these trenches do not present the same hostile appearance that would have been evident during the Great War. Gone were the straight edges and parapets; and left undisturbed for almost a century grass and naturalised wild flowers gave a softer less hostile appearance.

We walked down across No Mans Land, but always aware of the many shell holes, and visited Y Ravine Cemetery so immaculately maintained by The Commonwealth War Graves Commission. This was the first of many cemeteries we were to visit. Carrying on to the German trenches we looked up to the British Line as I tried to imagine the scene from the German's viewpoint. We continued past Y Ravine eventually arriving back at the British lines. This had been a poignant first afternoon on The Somme.

(Above)
Looking down across No Man's Land from the British Front

(Left)
The German Front

It was time to return to our guesthouse and prepare for evening meal and meet other guests. It appeared customary to meet each evening in the lounge, perhaps with a drink as conversation centred on individual reasons for visiting The Somme. Many like me were researching a family relative and their particular service within a variety of Regiments.

The original stable has been converted into the dining room; the manger and hayrack were retained. Photographs, maps and memorabilia from the Great War were displayed on all walls. Guests sat around one large table with Avril, talking about research connected with the area. After dinner most guests moved back to the lounge possibly with a drink as conversation continued, discussing that days visit or plans for next day. Avril had built up an extensive library of relevant books to help her guests with their research and to plan ahead.

We woke to heavy rain next morning, which cast some doubt on our planned visit to find Tombois Farm, along the Hindenburg Line. We were however not deterred and shortly after breakfast we first drove to Peronne. When crossing the River Somme I tried to imagine the scene there as the Battalion crossed via a temporary pontoon bridge marching towards their eventual objective, Tombois Farm.

Tombois Farm

My maps and local signposts did not always appear compatible but we eventually found the farm. It was isolated and appeared occupied but with many derelict buildings; the orchard still existed, but I assumed however that much had changed in 84 years.

Returning to Auchonvillers we first broke our journey in Peronne to visit the Historial De La Grande Guerre and spent an hour wandering through the various exhibition areas. We then visited Thiepval Memorial, standing nearly 150 feet high it dominates the surrounding area. On the sixteen pillars are engraved the names of over seventy-three thousand British and South African soldiers who fell on The Somme between 1 July 1916 and 20 March 1918, and still lie buried where they fell. They have no known grave.

Thiepval Memorial to the Missing on The Somme

After dinner that evening Avril invited guests down to the cellar and explained its history. No attempt had been made to change any aspect so it remains authentic. It was possible to see where bunk beds had been attached to the walls, and where soldiers had carved their names, or initials and Regiments on the walls.

The cellar beneath Avril Williams' Guesthouse

We returned to the comfort of the lounge to reflect on what we had seen, but found it difficult to comprehend what life would have been like for the injured and the doctors treating the wounded under appalling conditions.

The next morning we drove the short distance to Hébuterne to find the First Bucks Battalion Cemetery. I was aware that when my father and his mates first arrived at Hébuterne on The Somme in July 1915 a cemetery for those who lost their lives was created in the village. We found the cemetery in a quiet peaceful location on the outskirts of the village. While we were looking through the register we found reference to Private F J Coleman, his home was in Wingrave (next village to Aston Abbotts) He was killed in action on 1 April 1916. Undoubtedly my father would have known Fred, so we left a small British Legion cross and poppy on his grave.

(Above)
Hébuterne Cemetery

(Left)
Pte. Fred Coleman's grave

A short distance from Hébuterne is Gommecourt No. 2 Cemetery where we made a short break. As we were leaving a man whom I assumed to be a local resident approached me, and presented me with a small lapel badge, and said "Souvenir you" His knowledge of English was no better than my French so we were unable to communicate. However I did get the impression that he was pleased to hand me that gift.

Later that day I learned that these badges were made locally after the Great War and given in recognition of the help received from the allied forces during their hour of need. I felt very humble but extremely privileged to have received that gift, realising it really belonged to my father. He was there in 1915; I wasn't.

From there we drove to Albert, as I particularly wanted to visit the Musée des Abris. This museum was built in the subterranean tunnels under the Basilica and extended to other parts of the town. Both museums that we visited had different styles, but each presented their individual interests.

We strolled around the town past the Town Hall and Basilica before returning to Auchonvillers. We were always aware that our view of Albert was completely different from that my father and his mates would have known. As we arrived back early there was time for a cup of tea with Avril whilst talking about our day, and in particular the gift I received.

The next morning again started cloudy with showers. After breakfast we drove to Pozières, first visiting The Australian Memorial. Just across the road were the remains of the German Strongpoint "Gibraltar" and the adjacent raised platform provided excellent views across the battlefield.

Our next visit was Mouquet Farm (referred to by the Tommies as Mucky or Moo cow farm). During the Battle of The Somme the track opposite the farm was known as Skyline Trench (6 th Avenue) and was the scene of heavy fighting by the Battalion between 13 to 15 August 1916. Skyline trench eventually led into Warwick Avenue from where the Battalion was involved attacking the German outpost at Thiepval between 23 to 25 August 1916.

Looking across the Somme battlefield from the Australian Memorial

(Left)
Gibraltar Strongpoint at Pozières

A few miles further towards Bapaume we found Le Sars, another location where my father served. We then drove back along the main road to locate Destremont Farm, partly concealed within a copse. It was there that the Battalion took shelter whilst under heavy attack from the Le Sars area.

Continuing through Flers and Longueval we visited The South African Memorial and visitor centre at Delville Wood. There was insufficient time for a walk in the wood, which has been left untouched since the conflicts resulted in total devastation, although a gradual regeneration has evolved.

We continued on through Mametz and our next stop was La Boisselle and the Lochnagar Crater. This huge crater measuring 300 feet across and 90 feet deep was the result of 60,000 lbs. of ammonal detonated at 7.28 a.m. on 1 July 1916, the first day of the Battle of The Somme. It was awesome to stand looking across this crater. Private George Nugent who served with The Northumberland Fusiliers was one of those killed here; his body lay buried and undiscovered until the year 2000. His remains were identified from his dog tag, and an appeal was successful in locating his next of kin. On the anniversary of his death they attended his funeral when he was laid to rest with full military honours in Ovillers Military Cemetery. Tragically many bodies still lay undiscovered

The Lochnagar Crater at La Boisselle

The Lochnagar Crater Cross

We visited the cemeteries at Ovillers and Pozières, then returned to Auchonvillers in time for a cup of tea and discuss our day. Fine weather greeted us on Sunday morning; it was our last day on The Somme. Our time had passed quickly but I was now beginning to form a picture of my father's war. First we returned to Hébuterne to take a few more photographs, and then visited Sailly-au- Bois and Mailly-Maillet.

Our route back to Auchonvillers took us again to Pozières and we stopped at the military cemetery. I remembered that from one of the trench maps Sickle Trench stretched from the rear in an arc towards Ovillers. I walked to the rear and looked towards Ovillers but no evidence of the trench remained. From where I stood Thiepval Memorial was visible on the skyline. We drove back through Ovillers, Aveluy, and Beaumont making a brief detour to the sunken road at Beaumont Hamel.

Looking across the original site of Sickle Trench

We had spent four and a half days exploring The Somme and visited areas where my father and his mates had served. I have many memories of The Somme area but the sight of so many cemeteries represents the sacrifice of those who gave their lives. It still remains one of the greatest battles in history fought by the British Army.

***********

The next morning we left Auchonvillers and headed north and through Armentières into Belgium and Ypres. We checked in at our hotel in the Market Square.

During the afternoon we visited Cloth Hall and the museum, "In Flanders Fields." and the magnificent Cathedral. It was difficult to appreciate the scene here when the town was raised to the ground. After the war all the buildings around the square were rebuilt in their original style.

Looking across The Square towards Cloth Hall and The Cathedral

That evening we first went to The Shamrock restaurant, before visiting The Menin Gate for the Last Post Ceremony. Since 1928 except for the period during the Second World War that very moving ceremony has been performed at 8.00 p.m. every evening by buglers from the Ypres Fire Brigade. The ceremony is to express the town's eternal gratitude to the soldiers of The British Empire who fought and fell in defence of their town and the Ypres Salient. The pillars of this massive memorial are engraved with the names of 54,900 allied soldiers killed in the Ypres Salient and still lie buried where they fell.

Last Post ceremony at The Menin Gate

The next morning we drove back towards Armentières as far as Hyde Park Corner to visit Ploegsteert Wood. Walking along Mud Lane, now a solid path, we entered the wood near Mud Corner Cemetery. It was raining but we walked as far as Ploegsteert Wood Cemetery (1/1st Bucks burials) and to Rifle House Cemetery (1/4th Oxfords burials) The rain became more intense so we retraced our steps to Hyde Park Corner and The Auberge to dry out and have some refreshments.

Ploegsteert Wood Cemetery, 1/1st Bucks burials

Rifle House Cemetery, 1/4th Oxfords burials

While standing at the bar area I quickly became aware of a photograph displayed on the adjacent wall. It was of Stratford Road, Wolverton 1910, just a short distance from our home. My curiosity was aroused and I had to ask why the photograph was there. I discovered that in the adjacent Hyde Park Corner Cemetery is the grave of Private Albert French from Wolverton. Albert served with The Kings Own Rifle Corps and lost his life after just six weeks at the front. He was sixteen years old. This so touched the present Auberge proprietors, Claude and Nellie Verhaeghe-Lelue that it generated their interest in The Great War, leading them to become involved in pursuing the twinning of Ploegsteert with Wolverton.

Pte. Albert French's grave

The rain eased allowing us time to visit Hyde Park Corner cemetery to locate Albert French's grave. We left a small Royal British Legion cross and poppy, before visiting the Royal Berkshire Memorial opposite. During the afternoon we visited Hooge Crater cemetery, where 5924 soldiers were laid to rest, 3578 unknown.

We drove to Hill 62 (62 meters above sea level) and it quickly became evident why this position was so important. It allows extensive views across the flat landscape to Ypres and beyond.

Our afternoon concluded visiting Essex Farm, made famous by John McCrae author of the poem "In Flanders Fields" As a Lieutenant Colonel in the Canadian Medical Corps he operated a field dressing station just off the Ypres-Boezinge road. He later moved to a Military hospital in Boulogne. In 1918 the gas attacks he had previously endured affected his lungs and his health deteriorated; later a brain haemorrhage sadly led to his death on 28 January 1918, aged 45. He was laid to rest in Wimereux Military Cemetery just north of Boulogne.

We returned to Ypres with many memories of our first day in this area. That evening we decided to return to The Menin Gate earlier to ensure we were closer to the buglers, but were unaware that it was a special evening. Representatives from the Cork Fire Brigade were making a presentation to The Ypres Fire Brigade. The ceremony included the laying of wreathes, and the opportunity to meet and talk with several of the guests.

Whilst waiting for the buglers to march out, the evening was touched with sadness as we heard the news of the tragic terrorist attacks on The World Trade Centre in New York. It was not until the next morning that we learned of the devastation caused in New York and the loss of so many lives

For our visits the next day I planned first to look at the area around St Julien, a few miles north east of Ypres. For a while the Battalion's headquarters were in Alberta bunker, which had previously been a German Headquarters. Only a part of the bunker remained, but as I looked across the fields where cattle grazed I tried to imagine the scene in 1917 when the men existed there in glutinous mud.

(Left)
Alberta Bunker

Looking towards the 1/1st Bucks forming up positions 16 August 1917

We drove to Langemark to visit the German cemetery, which contains 44,292 burials, the bodies being exhumed from smaller cemeteries and now buried in mass graves. The surrounding trees and headstones made from a dark stone, and although laid flat gave this cemetery a sombre air. Most of those young men did not want to fight a war any more than of ours, and they must never be forgotten.

The German Cemetery at Langemark

Moving on we first visited Poelkapelle cemetery the final resting-place for almost 7000 soldiers, mostly unknown. We located the grave of Private W.W. Smith, 1/4th Oxfords, from Aston Abbotts who was killed in action on 20 September 1917 during The Third Battle of Ypres. I left a small British Legion cross and poppy.

Poelkapelle Cemetery contains the grave of the youngest U K soldier killed during the war; Private J Condon who served with the Royal Irish Regiment was killed in action 24 May 1915 during the Second Battle of Ypres. He was fourteen years old; volunteering as a boy but sadly died doing a man's job.

Pte W.W. Smith, 1/4th Oxfords

Pte J.Condon, Royal Irish Regt.

Within this cemetery are the graves side by side of seven men who served with the 48th Labour Company killed whilst clearing the cemetery after the war. When they lit a fire to cook a meal this triggered an explosion of a wartime shell.

Our return to Ypres took us close to Tyne Cot Cemetery so we decided to visit. Being the largest British Military Cemetery in the world it is difficult to describe one's first impression of 11,871 graves, particularly as 70% are of unknown soldiers. Row after row of headstones stand within this immaculately maintained cemetery remind the visitor of the sacrifices made by so many. Following a suggestion from King George V the Cross of Sacrifice was built over a German pillbox, allowing part of it to remain visible.

The perimeter walls are engraved with the names of almost 35,000 soldiers killed in The Ypres Salient and have no known grave; a continuation of those remembered on the Menin Gate.

It was from this area that the German bunkers and pillboxes visible across the skyline reminded the Northumberland Fusiliers of home and their Tyneside Cottages: hence the abbreviation to Tyne Cot.

(Right) Part of the original pillbox remains visible through the Cross of Sacrifice

Tyne Cot Cemetery

Just south of St Julien is Cheddar Villa, a German blockhouse captured by the Canadians; it was later used as the Regimental Aid Post, and our final stop. Whilst standing there I recalled it was in this blockhouse that a platoon from D Company was resting and suffered heavy casualties from a German shell landing inside. We returned to Ypres for our last night.

Cheddar Villa

The next morning we drove to Ostend for our return crossing to Dover. I had partly fulfilled my ambition to make that pilgrimage and visit some of the battlefield areas where my father served during The Great War.

***********

During September 2002 we visited Northern Italy and the densely forested mountains surrounding the Asiago Plateau. My first impression was of the different terrain between the mountains and the flat area of the Ypres Salient and the gently undulating area of The Somme in Picardy.

We arrived in Asiago at about 12.45 p.m. and checked into Hotel Alpi. The proprietor Sr. Marco Ambrosini was chairman of the local Italian Infantry Association and has some knowledge of English making limited conversation possible. After a light meal in The Al Sole (The Sun) restaurant we visited the tourist office and met Stefania with whom I had previously corresponded. Our visit to Asiago coincided with a visit by Richard Jeffs and his daughter Vicky. Richard was volunteer archivist at the Regimental Museum in Oxford and had previously provided information on The Somme, Ypres and Asiago all relevant to my research. He offered to accompany Jean and I around the battlefield sites where my father and his fellow soldiers fought in the mountains. We returned to our hotel for a siesta and to unpack.

Next morning we met Richard and Vicky as arranged. However during our visit to the Tourist Office the previous afternoon we learned of special events in Asiago planned for the afternoon that day, so we postponed our visits to the battlefield sites. The town was celebrating the re-opening of the road leading up to the Sacrario Militare (War Memorial) after restoration and the twinning of Asiago with Tempio Pausania in Sardinia.

Asiago War Memorial

During the morning Jean and I visited the Sacrario Militare. This imposing memorial is constructed of locally mined white marble and stands prominent on a hill overlooking the town. The inauguration ceremony in July 1937 was presided over by Mussolini. Walls of the corridors within the memorial form burial niches where the remains of 33,086 Italian soldiers are laid to rest, the identities of 20,291 are unknown. These bodies were exhumed from thirty-five different war cemeteries spread over the highlands.

Some years later the remains of 18,565 Austro-Hungarian soldiers (12,355 unknown) were buried here. Throughout the extensive corridors the walls are inscribed with the names of the fallen. Steps outside lead up to a terrace affording panoramic views of Asiago and beyond to mountains and battlefield areas. The British fallen still lie buried in secluded cemeteries located within the densely forested mountains.

Looking south across No Man's Land towards the British Front

Having previously discussed an itinerary with Richard next morning we drove from Asiago through Canove turning left on to a track at Ghelpac Fork. Shortly after passing under a narrow railway arch we first climbed onto a disused railway line and walking back across the bridge we stopped at Pelly trench. This area and trench have remained untouched since being the scene of ferocious fighting eighty-four years earlier. Although the line of the trench can be followed meandering through the woods it has become partly silted up over the years and does not present the hostile picture it once did, despite parts of the original barbed wire entanglements still being evident. Opposite Pelly Trench are the remains of the machinegun post hewn out of the rock and from where a tunnel led into Pelly Trench.

Princes Road from the Railway Arch

Moving along Princes Road past the Sunken Lane and Lemerle Switch trench we stopped at Boscon Cemetery. I located the grave of my father's cousin Albert Kent killed in action during the night of 15/16 June 1918 and frequently referred to as "The Battle in the Woods". I left a small British Legion cross and poppy on his grave, realising that I was possibly the first member of Albert's family to visit his grave.

Boscon Cemetery

Carrying on past the site of Swiss Cottage to our right (originally a field hospital) we visited Handley Cross, site of the infamous ammunition dump that exploded when hit by a shell on 15 June 1918.

We retraced our steps past Boscon Cemetery then along the Sunken Lane, first stopping at the site of the 1/4th Oxfords headquarters and dugout to our left. Carrying on we visited Lemerle Switch, Boscon Switch and the front line occupied by the 1/1st Bucks and 1/4th Oxfords during the 15 and 16 June 1918. Again I thought of the extreme difficulties that this densely wooded mountain terrain would have presented when fighting a war.

266613
Pte Albert Kent

Continuing on Richard pointed out various landmarks as we headed towards the site of the Division's outpost overlooking the Asiago Plateau. When viewing the plateau from there it quickly became apparent why this was such an important area to be chosen as an observation post. The Austro-Hungarian line traversed the foothills opposite, just south of Asiago and towards Canove. It was a peaceful day whilst we were there and our only company were two cows quietly grazing.

Looking north across the Asiago Plateau from the British Outpost

Retracing our steps to the car, we first made a detour to the area where in July 1918 the outstanding bravery of Second-Lieutenant Youll, 11th Battalion Northumberland Fusiliers earned him the Victoria Cross. He was later awarded the Italian Silver Medal for valour, but sadly killed in action a few weeks later. Returning to Asiago we stopped to visit the museum in Canove. Sunday had by tradition become the day when the local population congregated en mass in Asiago, and the main street attracted many people. Until The Great War the main street in Asiago was named Via Capovilla, but after rebuilding following the Armistice on 4 Novembre 1918 the street was aptly renamed Corsa IV Novembre.

As Monday was our last day we planned to spend it quietly. We had been very fortunate that our visit coincided with Richard's giving us the opportunity to obtain his knowledge and guidance.

When leaving next morning I again tried to envisage my father's life during the Great War. Each of the battlefield areas where he and his mates served provided their own individual characteristics, problems and dangers. I contrasted the comparative flat terrain of the Ypres Salient with the gently undulating battlefield areas of the Somme in Picardy. Finally I reflected upon the densely forested mountains surrounding the Asiago Plateau, where danger lurked behind every tree.

**I wonder what my father would have told us.**